Polls and Politics

Polls and Politics

The Dilemmas of Democracy

Edited by
Michael A. Genovese and Matthew J. Streb

STATE UNIVERSITY OF NEW YORK PRESS

Published by
State University of New York Press, Albany

Printed in the United States of America

For information, address State University of New York Press,
90 State Street, Suite 700, Albany, NY 12207

Production by Diane Ganeles
Marketing by Michael Campochiaro

Library of Congress Cataloging-in-Publication Data

Polls and politics : the dilemmas of democracy / edited by Michael A. Genovese and Matthew J. Streb
p. cm.
Based on a conference held at Loyola Marymount University in February 2002.
Includes bibliographical references and index.
ISBN 0-7914-6083-5 (alk. paper) — ISBN 0-7914-6084-3 (pbk. : alk. paper)
1. Democracy—United States. 2. Political participation—United States. 3. Public opinion—United States. 4. Public opinion polls. I. Genovese, Michael A. II. Streb, Matthew J. (Matthew Justin), 1974–

JK1726.P653 2004
320.973—dc22

2003059024

10 9 8 7 6 5 4 3 2 1

This book is dedicated to our wives,
who love us, understand us, and tolerate us.

To Page, with love, Matt
To Gaby, with love, Michael

Contents

Tables and Figures

Preface

This book stems largely from a conference held at Loyola Marymount University (LMU) in February 2002. Each President's Day, the LMU Institute for Leadership Studies convenes a conference on the overall theme Dilemmas of Democracy. The first conference focused on polling and democracy, and was headed by Matt Streb. Top scholars from around the country came together to discuss whether polling strengthens or undermines democracy. Academic papers were presented, and the participants had the opportunity to exchange ideas on this important and controversial topic.

We wish to thank a number of people who helped both this book and the conference become a reality. First, Loyola Marymount University provided us with a wonderful venue for the conference. The president of the university, Fr. Robert Lawton, graciously hosted the conference. Dr. Joseph Jabbra, academic vice president, and Dr. Kenyon Chan, dean of the Bellermine College of Liberal Arts, were indefatigable in their support, financial and otherwise. And this conference benefited greatly from having an amazing student assistant who ran everything, kept us on our toes, and corrected all our mistakes: Caroline Guidi. Caroline was also extremely helpful with formatting the book and tracking down references. We wish to thank Governor Michael Dukakis, who attended the conference and gave the keynote address at the conference dinner. It was a pleasure working with Michael Rinella and the people at SUNY Press as well. Finally, we wish to thank the conference participants for making the conference such a success. It was their insight and challenging perspectives that engaged the conference attendees and will, we are quite sure, engage the readers of this book.

For those of us committed to making democracy work, facing the complex role of polling in a democracy must be a central concern. Good polls, used well, can be an essential ingredient in a robust democracy. Bad polls or polling data improperly used can undermine and discredit democracy. How to execute the delicate tightrope walk is one of the key dilemmas of our government. This book looks unflinchingly at this controversy and tries to underline why polls strengthen democracy, but also why, because of unethical pollsters and an inability for the public and the media to analyze polls, they can undermine it.

Democracies are complex and messy. They were not meant to be efficient. A strong democracy requires much of leaders *and* citizens. It is our hope that this book can assist both leader and citizen in sorting out the strengths and weaknesses of polling in this democractic republic.

1

Polling and the Dilemmas of Democracy

Matthew J. Streb
and
Michael A. Genovese

On 21 January 1998, news media across the country became captivated by yet another alleged Clinton scandal, one that seemed more sensationalized and damaging than those of the past. Rumors quickly spread about a possible sexual relationship between Clinton and a young White House intern. Stories of Clinton's womanizing were not new, but because this was the first time Clinton had been accused of having an affair *as president*, this story had a greater impact. Clinton was accused of telling the intern, Monica Lewinsky, to lie under oath about the relationship. The allegations, if true, were quite serious. Even longtime Clinton advisor George Stephanopoulos, one of his most ardent supporters, said on ABC News that if the allegations were true, they could lead to impeachment proceedings.[1]

Clinton received advice from many people regarding how to handle the allegations. Some of Clinton's top advisors, including former chief of staff Leon Panetta and the chief of staff at the time, Erskine Bowles, told Clinton to come clean and take responsibility if the allegations were true.[2] Clinton did not listen to the advice of Panetta and Bowles. Instead, he relied on a longtime confidant, campaign strategist, and pollster, the controversial political consultant Dick Morris. Morris told the president to authorize a poll to gauge the reaction of the American public to the allegations; Clinton agreed. The poll indicated that the public was less concerned about the affair, but quite worried about the obstruction of justice charges.[3] As Stephanopoulos put it, "The poll said lie" if the charges were true.[4] Five days later, in the Roosevelt

Room of the White House, Bill Clinton, with a fixed glare, stared into a television camera, wagged his index finger, and emphatically insisted "I want you to listen to me . . . I did not have sexual relations with that woman, Miss Lewinsky. I never told anybody to lie. Not a single time. Never."[5]

As he did quite often with policy issues, Bill Clinton relied on a poll to help formulate his "position" on the Lewinsky scandal. According to presidential scholar George Edwards, "The Clinton administration is the ultimate example of the public presidency, one based on a perpetual campaign and fed by public opinion polls, focus groups, and public relations memos."[6] Clinton was notorious for taking into account public opinion on everything from health care to where he should spend his summer vacation. Critics claimed that Clinton relied too heavily on polls to formulate his policy views. According to Morris, the president was better at reading polls than any pollster Morris knew.[7]

With Clinton in his hottest water yet, the Republican-led Congress pursued impeachment. While Clinton looked to public opinion polls to formulate his message, Congress virtually ignored the public's attitudes on the scandal. Public opinion polls overwhelmingly indicated that, though the public did not condone the president's actions, they did not believe he should be impeached. Instead, nearly every poll showed that the public favored censure.[8] And yet, on 19 December 1998, William Jefferson Clinton became the second president in United States history to be impeached.

The two cases above show the importance—or perhaps lack of importance—of polls in American politics. The issue this book sets out to address is: what is the role of polls in a representative democracy? On the one hand, polls seem essential to the functioning of a robust democratic government. Some argue that polls are quintessential in a democracy because they send a symbolic message that the people matter. Proponents of polls suggest that, in a democracy, publicly elected officials should not only respond to the "will" of the people, but are obligated to follow the lead of the people and "give them what they want." Polls are one way to find out what the people want. Not only do polls provide politicians with the "will" of the people, but, as Asher notes, polls provide "the opportunity for citizens to learn about their compatriots and to dispel myths and stereotypes that might otherwise mislead public discourse."[9]

On the other hand, some people believe that politicians rely too heavily on polls—especially polls that may provide misleading or inaccurate information. Critics of polls assert that politicians often blindly follow polls when creating policy and fail to exert creative leadership. Others claim that pollsters have the potential to manipulate public opinion and the political agenda. Additionally, some have argued that polls have lessened voter turnout and created a more cynical public. Do polls make our government stronger by giving the citizenry a voice in the political process and providing important information about policies, campaign strategy, and the horse race? Or do they hinder and undermine democracy by forcing politicians to become slaves to the opinions of a generally uneducated public, allow for the manipulation of public opinion, and provide false information that has the ability to influence policy and electoral outcomes?

Whatever the answers to the above questions, Americans cannot escape polls; they are part of our everyday lives. We take polls on everything, from the presidential vote choice, to positions on abortion, to what movie should win the Oscar. During the 1996 presidential election alone, more than three hundred national and four hundred state polls asked voters for their presidential vote choice; this in an election that was not even close.[10] According to Traugott, eighteen different organizations produced a final estimate of the outcome in the 2000 presidential election and pollsters conducted more polls than ever before.[11] Since we cannot escape polls, we must understand their impact on our society.

Polling in a Democratic Society

This book sets out to analyze two different questions regarding polling and its place in a democratic society. First, how are polls used—or how should they be used—by policymakers, in this case, the president? Second, is polling dangerous to democratic governments or is it an essential aspect of democracies?

Politicians' Use of Polls

In a republic such as the United States, citizens elect representatives to go to Washington, state capitals, or city halls to make policy. Some believe that the role of an elected official is to act as a "delegate," to follow the will of the people when creating that policy. In a delegate version of democracy, if the people want tax cuts, the politicians should give them tax cuts. If not, come the next election the incumbents should be looking for new jobs. If one supports the delegate model of representation, then it is important for politicians to be able to read public opinion on a variety of issues. Polls can provide politicians with an estimation of popular will and sentiment. As Archibald Crossley wrote nearly seventy years ago, polls are "the long-sought key to 'Government *by* the people.'"[12] Beyond giving elected officials a sense of public opinion, polls send a symbolic message that the voice of the people matters.[13]

Politicians often decry the use of public opinion polls, arguing that they provide inaccurate information. Many elected officials claim they can read the political pulse of the people through meetings with constituents and phone calls and letters to their offices. However, the problem with relying entirely on these kinds of contacts is that politicians are unlikely to get an accurate picture of public opinion. The types of people who attend political rallies or write their congressperson look quite different than the public at large. It is the public at large that elects the politicians. Therefore, according to a delegate theory of representation, like it or not, politicians need public opinion polls.

Certainly not everyone believes in the delegate model of representation. Instead, many people take a Burkean view of representation. Under this model, politicians are not expected to follow public sentiment, but to act as "trustees" instead. Proponents of trustee representation believe that politicians should not vote with public opinion, but with their personal convictions about what they feel is best for their constituents or the country. We elect representatives not to use our judgment, but to use theirs; we elect them to apply their wisdom to the issues at hand. In other words, if the public wants tax cuts, but the politician knows that tax cuts will threaten Social Security, then the politician should vote against tax cuts. As "experts" on policy, politicians are believed to have a clearer idea of the impact of policy; therefore we entrust them to make the right decision. Several studies have indicated that politicians view themselves more as trustees than as delegates, although most prefer to act as "politicos," a mixture of the two models.[14] Interestingly, the public does not necessarily agree with the elites. A recent poll found that 63% of the public wanted Congress to "stick closely to American public opinion . . . including results of polls" when making legislative decisions. Only 34% wanted representatives to "do what they think is best."[15]

Nevertheless, many argue that politicians should pay little attention to polls, because they believe that polls do not provide any meaningful information about preferences. Scholars have long criticized the American voter for their lack of knowledge about politics and their inability to hold stable opinions.[16] In fact, Converse argued that the majority of Americans were incapable of thinking ideologically or holding consistent opinions on issues; instead, they held "non-attitudes."[17] A non-attitude is when people have no genuine opinion on an issue, yet respond to a survey question as if they do, so as not to look uneducated. The problem of non-attitudes can be immense because, if the public or even a portion of the public does indeed hold non-attitudes yet responds to a survey, we are not measuring opinions at all. In reality, all public opinion polls would indicate then would be a bunch of noise. In chapter 8, James Fishkin tackles the problem of non-attitudes head-on by arguing that deliberative polling is important for a healthy democracy.

While the delegate vs. trustee debate normally refers to legislators, perhaps no elected official faces more headaches regarding the role of public opinion than the President of the United States. As Michael Genovese discusses in chapter 2, the president is put in a precarious situation; we expect the president to lead, but at the same time we expect him to follow. We expect the president to do what we want, but we criticize the president, as we did Clinton, when he puts too much emphasis on public opinion polls. Because of this predicament, presidents spend a great deal of time trying to manipulate public opinion and have increasingly relied on polls.[18] In chapter 3, Larry Jacobs and Melinda Jackson provide an in-depth examination of Richard Nixon's use of polling, specifically his efforts to change the public's perception of his image and rally support for his administration. Diane Heith continues the discussion of presidents and polls in chapter 4 by examining presidents' use of polling from Nixon through George W. Bush. Heith argues that the president's use of polls to "permanently campaign" rather than to govern weakens the policymaking process.

The Dangers of Polling in a Democracy

Politicians certainly rely on polls for a variety of reasons—whether it is to help formulate strategy, decide where to stand on issues, or manipulate public opinion—but not everyone is enamored with the use of polls. In fact, many worry that polls actually undermine democracy.

While some question whether we want politicians following public opinion polls (because of the public's lack of knowledge regarding many issues and the possible presence of non-attitudes), perhaps the most common argument against the use of polls is that the "polls are wrong"; they lack external validity. The belief is that poll results are not generalizable. After all, as critics of polls argue, how can the opinions of fifteen hundred people tell us anything? Or, how accurate can polls be if I have never participated in one? The response to these questions is that statistical theory allows us to get a clear picture of what public opinion is without having to interview everyone. As Asher correctly notes, just as a chef does not have to eat the entire stew to determine if it is finished, pollsters do not have to interview the entire population to get an accurate reading of public opinion.[19]

Still, many people remain skeptical. Polls certainly are not always correct; even those that are perfectly implemented may have some problems (e.g., a bad sample). Others worry about the ability of polling results to be easily manipulated through question wording or the order the questions are asked. For instance, public opinion is drastically different when people are asked if they support *welfare* or *assistance to the poor*. Both questions get at the same topic—the government's role in helping the poor—but people are much more likely to favor "assistance to the poor" than they are "welfare."[20]

One area where polls receive great criticism is their ability to correctly predict the winner of an election. In reality, since the 1950s trial heat polls have been quite accurate in predicting the winner of presidential elections. Polls become even more precise the closer they are conducted to Election Day.[21] Since 1952, the average error in the final Gallup Poll has been less than 2%.[22] Occasionally, the polls have not correctly predicted the winner (e.g., many of the final polls in 2000 forecasted that Bush would win the popular vote) or they have overestimated the margin of victory (e.g., Clinton in 1992), but these examples are not common.

Exit polls—where voters are asked whom they voted for as they leave the voting booth—in particular are the subject of skepticism by the public, especially given the controversy surrounding the 2000 presidential election. In chapter 7, Jerry Wright argues that the public's concerns over the accuracy of exit polls, while perhaps understandable in light of recent events, are not valid. In fact, Wright claims that exit polls are beneficial in a democracy because they allow researchers to understand certain phenomena, such as why people voted the way that they did.

Polls also provide candidates with important information. They allow candidates to see their standing in the horse race, learn where they are strong and where they are weak, and help them create campaign messages and develop strategy. Imagine being a student where you received no feedback on your performance until the last day of class. You would not know if you should keep doing what you have been doing or needed to take a different approach. Feedback on exams provides you with that information. Polls are the "midterms" for candidates.

While the polls may be accurate, the public still could be receiving inaccurate information. Many question the media's ability to interpret polls. Michael Traugott argues in chapter 5 that journalists play a crucial role in acting as intermediaries between the polling organizations and the people, but they are not always trained in interpreting polls.[23] As Traugott shows, the results of the same poll are often read differently by various media sources. The problem is exacerbated by the fact that the public often blindly follows what the media are reporting as truth. This faith often occurs because the public, like the media, is not educated on distinguishing between a good poll and a bad one, nor is it trained in interpreting poll results.

As Traugott notes, the media's discussion of polls could also have an effect on political behavior. Studies of media coverage during elections have found that it is often the horse race that gets the most attention.[24] On the one hand, the media's constant discussion of the polls could be positive. While Americans are not necessarily active consumers of politics, they seem to enjoy the competitive aspect of politics; therefore, polls could spark political interest and participation. According to Lavrakas and Traugott, polls can engage citizens in the political process and raise their interest in elections.[25] Americans love competition; they want to know who is winning and who is losing. Polls provide this information. In turn, they may allow citizens to become more educated on certain elections and the issues involved. Lavrakas and Traugott are quick to point out, however, that the use of polls has a downside if the discussion is simply the horse race.

Not everyone buys the claim that polls spark interest and turnout. In fact, some believe just the opposite. In 1996, Roper Center director Everett Carll Ladd was quite critical of polls overstating Bill Clinton's margin of victory over Bob Dole.[26] He argued that the fact that the polls predicted an easy Clinton victory dampened interest in the election, causing lower voter turnout (turnout in the 1996 election was the lowest since 1924). Traugott briefly addresses this question in chapter 5.

Similar criticism has been directed toward exit polls. Some scholars claim there is an East Coast bias to exit polls that lessens turnout on the West Coast,[27] although not everyone agrees.[28] For instance, in 1980 early exit poll results from states in the eastern time zone clearly indicated a Reagan landslide. As a result of the exit poll returns, Jimmy Carter had already conceded the election at 9:30 P.M. eastern standard time, while polls in some western states were still open for another hour and a half. Though the early calls did not influence the outcome of the presidential election, they may have affected local races by keeping voters on the West Coast away from the polls. Reagan certainly still would have won, but his margin of victory might have been smaller, and Democrats might have fared better in state and local elections.

The controversy surrounding exit polls in the 2000 presidential election brought a different charge regarding voter turnout. There was controversy because the networks had called Florida for Al Gore before all of the precincts in the state had finished voting. Because the Florida panhandle is in the central time zone, precincts were still open in the largely Republican part of the state when the networks had already declared Gore the winner. Republican leaders claimed that this action by the media had an influence on the outcome in Florida because it discouraged Republicans in the panhandle from voting. "Every single state that was called for Gore was called sooner, much sooner, than the states that were called for Bush," complained Rep. Billy Tauzin (R-LA.).[29]

Not only can polls potentially influence *whether* someone votes, people argue they also influence *how* someone votes. There are two hypothesized effects that occur because of the information citizens receive from trial heat polls: the bandwagon effect and the underdog effect. Forget polls for a minute and think about the NCAA basketball tournament. Many people who have little interest in who wins the tournament before it begins suddenly find themselves rooting for a team. They may support a team that is expected to do well—jump on the bandwagon—because that is the popular choice. Or, they might find themselves rooting hard for "the little guy." We often love an upset; we want to see the underdog do well. Some scholars argue that the same phenomenon occurs in elections, or at least there is some evidence that it is likely to be present.[30] People may see that a candidate has a comfortable lead and identify with the winner, or they might pull for the underdog. Either way, the voting behavior of citizens could be influenced by the polls. Not everyone believes that bandwagon and underdog effects are as prominent as some scholars suggest. Asher claims that there is a lack of evidence supporting either of these views. "Bandwagon and underdog effects can and do occur," writes Asher, "but their magnitude is small and probably inconsequential."[31] However, Sabato and Simpson argue that whether there is actually a bandwagon effect is of little importance. "There may actually be little or no real 'bandwagon effect,'" write the authors, "but politicians and consultants *believe* there is such a thing and strive to create it by looking like a winner."[32] In other words, candidates may try to manipulate trial heat polls.

Manipulation of trial heat polls is not the only concern regarding polling. People also worry about the manipulation of public opinion in general. We noted earlier Jacobs and Jackson's study of Nixon in chapter 3. However, the problem of manipulation could be much more deceitful than the tactics employed by Nixon. In chapter 6, Matt Streb and Susan Pinkus discuss various types of unscientific or unethical polls and the problems these polls can potentially create. Streb and Pinkus focus primarily on one particular kind of devious polling: push polls. These "polls" are not really polls at all. Instead, respondents are presented with hypothetical, often blatantly false information under the guise of legitimate survey research. As Streb and Pinkus argue, these polls lead people to question legitimate survey research, they manipulate public policies, and they have the potential to make people cynical about politics. It is not that Streb and Pinkus are arguing that polling is bad—in fact, like Traugott, they believe that when conducted properly polls can be extremely useful and important in a democracy—but that we must be concerned that polls are implemented and interpreted properly.

While most of the scholars in this book argue that, even with the potential problems of polls, they are an integral part of any robust democracy, the public may not agree. Traugott found that the public believes that polls are accurate estimates of the outcome, but that they did not like the "intrusiveness of the continual presentation of the 'trial heat' results."[33] This finding reminds one of us of our grandmother who would refuse to participate in trial heat polls. When asked whom she would be voting for, her reply was always, "I thought the ballot was supposed to be secret." The public seems to hold opinions similar to grandma's. According to one poll, 66% of respondents felt that the media spent too much time discussing pre-election polling stories in the 1988 presidential election.[34]

Because of the controversy surrounding exit polls, the public's disdain for them is even more intense. According to Traugott, a majority (51%) believe that the "government should not allow early election projections."[35] Lavrakas, Holley, and Miller came to similar conclusions.[36] In chapter 7, Jerry Wright goes into greater detail regarding this subject, arguing that, even though the people do not like them, exit polls have an important place in a democratic society.

The History of Polling in America

Concerns regarding polling are not new; people have criticized polls since they were first conducted. In fact, polling has been around for quite some time. It is generally agreed that 1824 was the first presidential election in which polls were used. In that election, the

Harrisburg Pennsylvanian conducted a "straw poll" (a poll that does not use probability sampling) that showed Andrew Jackson leading John Quincy Adams 335 votes to 169.[37] Other newspapers and some magazines, such as the *Farm Journal*, began producing straw polls during the nineteenth century. However, it was not until 1916 that presidential trial-heat polls received extensive coverage. That year, the *Literary Digest* conducted the first of several polls trying to predict the winner of the presidential election. The *Digest* correctly forecasted the winner of the 1916, 1920, 1924, 1928, and 1932 elections, although the predictive power of the poll was somewhat limited outside of forecasting the winner.[38] In 1936, the magazine predicted that Kansas Governor Alfred Landon would beat incumbent President Franklin Roosevelt in a landslide. In reality, Landon won only two states and a total of eight electoral votes. What went wrong? The *Literary Digest*'s sample was biased toward the Republican Landon. The people included in the sample were chosen from telephone directories and automobile registrations. With the country still in the midst of its greatest depression ever, the people on these lists were overwhelmingly wealthy Republicans. A class bias skewed the results.

The unscientific nature of the *Literary Digest* poll brought about more scientific ways to predict presidential elections by polling luminaries such as George Gallup, Elmo Roper, and Archibald Crossley. The new wave of pollsters were embarrassed in 1948 when they predicted that New York Governor Thomas Dewey would defeat incumbent President Harry S Truman. The blunder led to one of the most recognizable pictures for students of American politics: Truman holding up a copy of the *Chicago Tribune* that had the headline "Dewey Defeats Truman." While pollsters had made great strides in the twelve years since the *Literary Digest*'s error, they still had to develop better polling techniques. Pollsters had difficulty predicting who would actually vote in the election. Their sampling methods remained inadequate, and they did not conduct polls until Election Day. Because the Dewey-Truman race was believed to be a blowout, some polling organizations stopped conducting polls as early as September! The failure to poll closer to Election Day kept pollsters from capturing voters who made up or changed their minds in the last several weeks of the campaign. As noted earlier, since the Dewey-Truman race, pollsters have been much more accurate in their predictions. With the greater predictive power of trial heat polls today, pollsters and news organizations are conducting more polls than ever before.

While polling to predict election winners has been around for quite some time, politicians' use of polls to measure public opinion is relatively new. Certainly, as Genovese argues in chapter 2, presidents have always tried to measure the pulse of public opinion, but presidents were forced to rely on unscientific methods such as afternoon "open houses" where citizens were encouraged to visit the White House to discuss their concerns with the president. It was not until John Kennedy that presidents regularly polled public opinion in scientific ways, although FDR did encourage the development of government polling.[39] Kennedy's internal polls were kept quite secret, however, to keep people from thinking that he was creating policy based on public opinion polls.[40] As Jacobs and Jackson note in chapter 3, Nixon was really the first president to continuously commission public opinion polls. Heith discusses in chapter 4 how presidents' reliance on polls has not changed with Bill Clinton or George W. Bush.

Polling has come a long way, then. Whether polling to predict elections or polling to govern, the quality of polling has improved and the importance of polling has grown immensely. As a result, the number of polls conducted has exploded. Like it or not, polling has become a part of the everyday lives of Americans, and it is not going to go away anytime soon. Since we cannot escape polling, we might as well learn to understand it. Accordingly, this book sets out to analyze what the place of polling is and should be in a robust democracy.

The Format of the Book

This book addresses whether polls make democracies stronger or whether they undermine democracy. The following chapters focus on the two main questions posed above: How do policymakers use polls? And what are the dangers of polling in a democracy? Chapters 2–4 examine the importance of polling and public opinion as they relate to political actors—in this case, the president of the United States. In chapter 2, Michael Genovese notes the problems presidents have when trying to govern. On the one hand, presidents are expected to lead. We want persuasive presidents who feel strongly about a platform and are able to rally the public around their cause. We do not want presidents who continually succumb slavishly to the will of the people. At the same time, presidents are expected to follow "our lead." We become leery of presidents who try to manipulate public opinion, and we negatively rate presidents when they take unpopular positions. In chapter 3, Larry Jacobs and Melinda Jackson examine Richard Nixon's use of polling to attempt to manipulate perceptions of the president. In chapter 4, Diane Heith concludes the discussion of polling and the president by analyzing polling in the Nixon through Bush II administrations. Heith argues that recent presidents have continually used polls to "permanently campaign."

In chapter 5, the discussion moves away from the president and instead focuses on the public. Mike Traugott asks the question: "Do Polls Give the People a Voice in a Democracy?" Traugott asserts that people know little about accepted polling methods and that this lack of knowledge limits the public's ability to analyze poll results. He also takes the media to task (specifically journalists) for its poor understanding of poll results and argues that this can distort the public's perceptions of what public opinion really is on various subjects.

In chapter 6, Matt Streb and Susan Pinkus examine nonscientific and unacceptable forms of polls, including push polls. Streb and Pinkus maintain that these types of unscientific polls are dangerous in a democracy because they distort true public opinion and have the potential to make people cynical about polling and politics. Unfortunately, these polls have become more prominent in the last several years and show little sign of dissipating.

In chapter 7, Jerry Wright makes a strong argument favoring the use of exit polls. Wright claims that the public misunderstands exit polls. Instead of exit polls being a negative in a democratic government by possibly influencing the outcomes of elections, Wright asserts that they are imperative because they provide valuable information to the public, the media, and researchers.

In chapter 8, Jim Fishkin discusses his attempts to diminish the problems of "non-attitudes" through the use of deliberative polling. Fishkin argues that most polls provide inaccurate information because people do not have true opinions about the issues that they are asked. Deliberative polling improves democracy, Fishkin claims, by showing what "true" public opinion would be on issues if the public were informed. He believes that deliberative polling, in turn, will educate the public allowing them to make better decisions when voting.

Finally, in chapter 9, we close by arguing that polls, when conducted and interpreted correctly, do not undermine democracy. Instead, they are an essential part of any functioning representative government.

Notes

1. Stephanopoulos, *All Too Human*, p. 434.
2. Ibid., p. 436.

3. Heith, "Polling for a Defense."

4. Stephanopoulos, *All Too Human*, p. 436.

5. Brice, "Not a Single Time, Never," p. A1.

6. Edwards, "Frustration and Folly," p. 234.

7. Morris, *Behind the Oval Office*, p. 143.

8. Jacobs and Shapiro, *Politicians Don't Pander*.

9. Asher, *Polling and the Public*, 4th ed, p. 21.

10. Bogart, "Politics, Polls, and Poltergeists."

11. Traugott, "Assessing Poll Performance."

12. Crossley, "Straw Polls in 1936," p. 35.

13. Lavrakas and Traugott, *Election Polls, the News Media, and Democracy*.

14. Kuklinski and McCrone, "Electoral Accountability"; Friesma and Hedlund, "The Reality of Representational Roles."

15. Morin, "Unconventional Wisdom."

16. Campbell et al., *The American Voter*; Converse, "The Nature of Belief Systems."

17. Converse, "Attitudes and Non-attitudes."

18. Jacobs and Shapiro, *Politicians Don't Pander*.

19. Asher, *Polling and the Public*, 4th ed.

20. Rasinski, "The Effect of Question Wording."

21. Jones, *Who Will Be in the White House?*; Erikson and Wlezien, "The Timeline of Political Campaigns."

22. Wayne, *The Road to the White House 2000*.

23. One of the contributors to this book experienced the lack of the media's knowledge regarding polls at first hand. During a "prep" meeting with broadcasters to discuss the results of a local mayoral election, the contributor was asked if the exit poll results were raw numbers or percentages.

24. Lichter and Noyes, "There They Go Again"; Streb, *The New Electoral Politics of Race*.

25. Lavrakas and Traugott, *Election Polls, The News Media, and Democracy*.

26. Ladd, "The Election Polls."

27. Jackson, "Election Night Reporting."

28. Epstein and Strom, "Survey Research and Election Night Projections."

29. Walker, "Truth or Consequences," p. P1.

30. Goidel and Shields, "The Vanishing Marginals"; Ceci and Kain, "Jumping on the Bandwagon"; Navazio, "An Experimental Approach to Bandwagon Research"; Fleitas, "Bandwagon and Underdog Effects"; Lavrakas, Holley, and Miller, "Public Reactions to Polling."

31. Asher, *Polling and the Public*, 4th ed., p. 139.

32. Sabato and Simpson, *Dirty Little Secrets*, p. 247.

33. Traugott, "Public Attitudes about News Organizations," p. 143; see also Roper, "Evaluating Polls with Poll Data."

34. Lavrakas, Holley, and Miller, "Public Reactions to Polling."

35. Traugott, "Public Attitudes about News Organizations."

36. Lavrakas, Holley, and Miller, "Public Reactions to Polling."

37. Moon, *Opinion Polls*.

38. Crossley, "Straw Polls in 1936."

39. Jacobs, "The Recoil Effect."

40. Kennedy was so concerned about his use of polls that they were kept in a safe in the attorney general's office.

2

Presidents, Polls, and the Paradox of Democratic Governance

Michael A. Genovese

> People are unpredictable by nature, and although you can take a nation's pulse, you can't be sure that the nation hasn't just run up a flight of stairs, and although you can take a nation's blood pressure, you can't be sure that if you came back in twenty minutes you'd get the same reading.
>
> —E.B. White

Winston Churchill, commenting on the view that politicians ought to be highly attuned to public opinion (that is, "keep their ears to the ground") reminded us that "the British nation will find it very hard to look up to the leaders who are detected in that somewhat ungainly posture."

To lead, or to follow the will of the people; that is the question. Whether 'tis nobler to suffer the slings and arrows of being accused of defying the sacred will of public opinion or to defy it and in so doing, attempt to lead or move the public.

Presidents often find themselves in no-win situations: damned if they do, damned if they don't; caught between a rock and a hard place. Nowhere is the dilemma of presidential governance more visible than in the relationship between a president and public opinion.

Should a president "lead" or "follow"? Should a president push and pull the public toward his vision, or should he attempt to discern where the public wants to go, and facilitate the achievement of the public's goals and preferences? Is the president an echo chamber of public opinion, or a shaper of opinion? Is the president a barometer or a leader?

In a democracy, is the voice of the people the voice of God? Do we elect a president to do "our" bidding, or to make decisions, choices, and lead?

How do presidents use poll data? How should they? And in a democracy, what is the proper connection between leadership and responsiveness? These questions are especially troublesome in a democracy, for there is an inevitable tension between presidential leadership and responsiveness. When and under what circumstances should a president attempt to lead? When should he follow?

All this begs the question: Is there—can there be—such a thing as "democratic leadership"?

Thomas Jefferson and the Vision of Democratic Leadership

Democratic theorists have long wrestled with a particularly vexing question: Is there such a thing as "democratic leadership?" Or are the two words mutually exclusive, if not contradictory? Thomas E. Cronin has gone so far as to call them "warring concepts."[1] But can any system of government exist without leadership? For those who believe in the superiority of democracy over other forms of government, a way must be found to reconcile these two seemingly warring concepts into a sustainable whole.

The tension between the need for leadership and the demands of democracy was reinforced by James Bryce, who reminded us that "Perhaps no form of government needs great leaders so much as democracy."[2] But what kind of leadership? The strong, forceful direction of a heroic leader, or the gentle guiding hand of a teacher? Emile Zapata warned us that "Strong leaders make a weak people," but can the people come together and accomplish their goals with weak leadership?

Proponents of robust democracy realize, as Bruce Miroff wrote, that

> Leadership has rarely fit comfortably with democracy in America. The claim of leaders to political precedence violates the equality of democratic citizens. The most committed democrats have been suspicious of the very idea of leadership. When Thomas Paine railed against the "slavish custom" of following leaders, he expressed a democrat's deepest anxiety.[3]

But such tensions have not prevented Americans from looking to strong leaders to guide the republic. Especially during a crisis, we turn to our leaders in hopes that strong or heroic leadership can save the republic. Thus, while we are suspicious of strong leadership, we also admire and sometimes even hunger for it. As Arthur M. Schlesinger Jr. noted:

> The American democracy has readily resorted in practice to the very leadership it had disclaimed in theory. An adequate democratic theory must recognize that democracy is not self-executing: that leadership is not the enemy of self-government but the means of making it work; that followers have their own stern obligation, which is to keep leaders within rigorous constitutional bounds; and that Caesarism is more often produced by the failure of feeble governments than by the success of energetic ones.[4]

Dilemmas notwithstanding, is there a style of leadership compatible with political democracy? While a tension will always exist between leadership and democracy, there are ways to bring the two into a creative tension that both calls for a role for the leader while also promoting democratic participation and practices among the citizenry.

Just as Abraham Lincoln gave us a succinct definition of democracy as "government of the people, by the people, and for the people,"[5] so too did one of America's other Mt. Rushmore leaders give us an eloquent, even simple definition of democratic leadership. Thomas Jefferson believed that the primary duties of a leader in a democracy were "to inform the minds of the people, and to follow their will."[6]

There are two key concepts contained in Jefferson's brief definition: *inform minds* and *follow the people's will*. Informing the minds of the people speaks to the role of leader as educator. In a democracy, the leader has a responsibility to educate, enlighten, and inform the people. He or she must identify problems and mobilize the people to act. By informing or educating the citizenry the leader also engages in dialogue, the ultimate goal of which is to involve leader and citizen in the process of developing a vision, grounded in the values of the nation, which will animate future action.

The leader's task in a democracy is to look ahead, see problems, focus the public's attention on the work that must be done, provide alternative courses of action, chart a path for the future, and move the nation in support of these ideas. The leader must attempt to mobilize the public around a vision and secure a consensus on the proper way to proceed.

The second component of Jefferson's definition, to "follow their will," suggests that after educating and involving the people, the leader must ultimately listen to the people. Several commentators have noted the distinction between the whim of the people (temporary and changing) and the will of the people (deeply held truths that speak to the nation's highest aspirations). The leader's job is to inform, educate, and persuade the public to embrace and work for a vision, which taps into the deeper truths and higher purposes of the will of Americans. But whatever their judgment, the leader must serve the people, and ultimately follow their direction. Of course, this leaves little room for a "profile in courage" type of leader.

In a democracy, following the will of the people is essential. Any leader who pursues policies contrary to the expressed wishes of the public can be accused of the democratic cardinal sin: defying the will of the people. Thus, to be a leader requires that one do all one can to bring about informed judgments by the people. Then, the leader must *serve* the people. This form of democratic accountability calls for the leader to play an important role, but it ultimately relies upon the people to make final judgments.

Broken down into its core elements, the chief components of democratic leadership include:

- Moral vision
- Egalitarian goals
- Educative functions
- Empowerment
- Question and challenge citizens
- Dialogue with citizens
- Leader-citizens engagement
- Respect for citizens
- Rule of law
- Enabling-facilitating role
- Service to the public's will

The best of this type of leadership, in Bruce Miroff's words, "not only serves people's interests but furthers their democratic dignity as well."[7] Thus, Thomas Jefferson's vision of a democratic leadership that informs the public, then follows their will, elevates both leader and citizen. Such a form of leadership is difficult, time-consuming, and fraught with pitfalls. But it is a style of leadership that builds strong citizens for a strong democracy.

The Framers, the President, and the Voice of the People

> I wonder how far Moses would have gone if he'd taken a poll in Egypt? What would Jesus Christ have preached if he'd taken a poll in Israel? . . . It isn't polls or public opinion

> of the moment that counts. It is right and wrong leadership... that makes epochs in the history of the world.
>
> —Harry S Truman

The framers of the U.S. Constitution did not want the president to be a slave to public opinion. They wanted a statesman who would administer fairly based on the rule of law, not the whim of the people. In fact, they sought to insulate the president from the vagaries of public pressure. By not being directly elected, the president was, in a way, shielded from this pressure, and from the obligation to give the people what they wanted.

Of course, there was a time when considerations of public opinion and democratic styles of leadership meant little to rulers. In the Middle Ages in Europe, when the voice of the king was thought to be the voice of God, rulers spent precious little time worrying about how their policies would play in Peoria. The divine right of kings, however, gave way, as a result of the democratic revolutions in the United States and then in France in the eighteenth century, to the divine right of the people!

Decoupling power from religion undermined respect for authority by putting it on a more temporal ground—the will of the people. In secularizing power, authority shifted from God to the people, and thus appeals to the public for consensus and approval became the new guiding principle on which authority and legitimacy were based.

This marked a dramatic change from the divine right of kings. And despite efforts to the contrary by the framers of the U.S. Constitution, over time the insulation built around the presidents protecting them from the pressure of public opinion eroded and left presidents exposed and vulnerable to the public whim. As the nation democratized, so too did the presidency. And soon, starting with the presidency of Andrew Jackson,[8] presidents came to see the voice of the people not just as a restraint on action, but also as a potential source of power. Instead of the president rising above opinion, the president now claims to represent and speak for the public. The public, so presidents would have us think, speaks through the president, and he expresses their power.

From chief magistrate to tribune of the people: today we have a more Rousseauist conception of the president as representative and repository of the general will. This plebiscitary theory of the presidency, of course, still encounters the occasional resistance from the Madisonian checks and balances, but a president armed with the will of the people is hard to hold in check.

Presidents soon learned that meeting the demands and expectations placed upon their office and achieving their own goals and aspirations required more power than the office was constitutionally granted. Therefore, presidents had to devise extra constitutional ways to bridge this expectation/power gap. Jefferson became a leader of his party in Congress, Lincoln became a wartime commander, and Teddy Roosevelt exploited the bully pulpit. But it was Andrew Jackson who added "voice of the people" to the arsenal of presidential power.[9] This, of course, is not what the framers wanted. The plebiscite of today, where the president sits—so they claim—on the shoulders of the public, was deemed to be fraught with the danger of demagoguery.

The problem is that we have a Madisonian system requiring Hamiltonian energy to meet Jeffersonian ends and expectations! The system, with its separation of powers and its checks and balances, remains difficult to move. But the presidency of today—the focus of so many demands and so much attention—suggests a brand of Jeffersonian democracy where the people speak through the president. But it is not constitutionally so. This illustrates the contradiction between the presidency in the Constitution and the presidency in practice.

Arguing that the United States has become "more of a Jeffersonian direct democracy," the infamous political consultant Dick Morris asserts that a president's "functional strength ebbs and flows with his popularity as it is measured in weekly tracking polls," and that today's leader "does not just need public support to win elections; he needs it to govern."[10] This reliance on measuring as well as being empowered by the pulse of the public "has changed the very nature of our democracy,"[11] and so "Each day is Election Day in modern America."[12]

Morris is half right. Yes, we have entered an era, sometimes characterized as "hyperdemocracy," in which the president is susceptible to the vagaries of public opinion. But we still operate within a constitutional framework based on Madisonian principles that both empower and (more often) enchain a president.

To understand this duality, we must distinguish between the leadership *of* opinion and leadership *by* opinion. Leadership *of* opinion seeks to shape and educate public sensibilities; leadership *by* opinion seeks to be guided by the will of the people. Mere officeholders are not necessarily leaders. Leaders attempt to mold public views, educate the public, and set direction for the people. Clerks and mere officeholders are content to conform to the will of the people.

James MacGregor Burns described the dilemma of the leader or follower by telling the old story of the French politician who, on seeing a crowd of people hurrying down a street, says, "There goes the mob,

I am their leader, I must find out where they are going so I can lead them there." The paradox of leadership in a democracy is that leaders are expected to simultaneously lead *and* follow. These contradictory expectations—leadership and responsiveness—form the core dilemma forced on an officeholder who seeks both to lead the public but also be responsive to the will of the people. It is a tough balancing act.

How should politicians resolve a conflict between their deeply held views and (when it contradicts their views) the will of the people?

The Case for Responding

> Public opinion is the social judgment reached upon a question of general or civic import after conscious, rational discussion.
>
> —Clyde King

In a democracy, should not a president be *responsive* to, as he is *responsible* to, public opinion in forming policy? After all, it is not a king we are electing, but a constitutional president. Are not the people to direct this government of, by, and for the people? Is that not what democracy is all about?

While democracies are not self-executing, they do require that those elected by the people be responsive to their will. Why have a democracy if the will of the people can be easily ignored? For democracy to have any meaning, it must be responsive to the will of the people.

To not respond to the will of the people is to run the risk of being un- or anti-democratic—a cardinal sin in our system. No politician can exhibit deafness to the voice of the people and long remain in office.

The Case against Responding

> [T]here is no such thing as public opinion, and it only requires moderate understanding of human nature to show that such a thing as an intelligent public opinion is not possible.
>
> —E. Jordan

At what point does responsiveness degenerate into pandering? Some—many of them critics of democracy—argue that the public is largely uninformed, often uninterested, and overall, ill suited to govern. While these arguments are not new, they have taken on a new urgency in an age of hyperdemocracy.

The very term hyperdemocracy suggests a demand overload that the government cannot meet. As more groups place more demands on the government to do more for them, and as the elected officials respond to these demands, lest they suffer the risk of defeat at the next election, a budget-busting pressure leads to huge deficits— deficits that make it less likely for the government to meet the demands of future claimants. It is a vicious cycle. The leader who stands up to these demands does so at great risk.

The traditional Republican response to "gimmie" demands is to shower tax cuts on the public. The traditional Democrat response is to shower government programs. Either way, demand overload severely restricts the government's ability to respond appropriately to public policy problems.

Of Polls and Presidents

> In this and like communities, public sentiment is everything. With Public sentiment nothing can fail, without it nothing can succeed.
>
> —*Abraham Lincoln*

Presidents govern, or attempt to do so, from a position of some weakness. While they do not enter the political battle unarmed, there is a very real gap between demands and expectations (which are very high) on the one hand, and power (quite limited) that is shared.[13]

One potential source of power or influence is public support or popularity. While it is not always easy to convert popularity into power, it is clear that the absence of popular support means political weakness. Therefore, presidents must be constantly vigilant in trying to maintain popularity.

If popularity is a potential power resource,[14] and if presidents spend a great deal of time and effort attempting to boost their popularity, one can fairly ask: How malleable is opinion to efforts at presidential manipulation? Between 1953 and 1965 (excluding only 1958), the average yearly presidential Gallup poll approval rating hovered at 60% or better. But starting in 1966, roughly the time when the most recent era of "failed presidents" began, the level of popular support declined dramatically. Presidents who attained a 50% support level were unusual. In the age of failed leaders, the average yearly popularity of presidents has dropped roughly 10%. As public expectations for the heroic model of the presidency soared, a gap between what was expected and what was delivered helped create what might be called a "delivery gap." Greater expectations led to greater disappointments—no matter what presidents do, it isn't enough (e.g., Clinton's September 1994 agreement on Haiti met with as much criticism as praise). No wonder these presidents have a hard time leading.[15]

While public approval is the result of many factors, and while presidents can get a short-term boost in popularity during what are called "rally events" (e.g., international threats), it is also clear that over the long haul, popularity is the product of public judgments both over the way things are going generally and how the president is doing his job.[16]

Popularity or, more broadly, "prestige"—to use Neustadt's term—is shaped by a complex web of factors, but overall, the most important is the public's perception of the state of the economy.[17] The public will praise or blame the sitting president for the state of the economy, regardless of what a president does or does not do. Thus, when the economy is booming, presidential popularity rises; when the economy is in a down spiral, the president's popularity drops. Students of presidential popularity would do well to remember the advice posted on the wall of the Clinton campaign headquarters during the 1992 election: "It's the economy, stupid!" Candidate Clinton persistently focused attention on the sour state of the economy, knowing that George H. W. Bush (whether he deserved it or not) would be blamed for the slow economy.

If popularity equals (to an extent) power, and if efforts to manipulate levels of popular support are limited, presidents are caught between a rock and a hard place (the Bermuda Triangle of presidential politics). They must constantly be concerned with their popularity, and yet their ability to generate support is often out of their control.

Polls and popularity ratings "have altered the time frame of democratic government, from quadrennial election to monthly review."[18] They force the president to dance to a different and much faster tune. With one eye always focused on popularity, presidents may be less likely to make the tough choices, the hard decisions.[19] Flattering the public has a greater short-term benefit than speaking the truth.

The relationship between the president and the public he is to simultaneously serve and lead is a complex one. In order to govern, a president must have a fairly high level of popular support. But the avenues open to a president for attaining that support are limited. Public demands and expectations are high and often contradictory. The public wants presidents to deliver good news, not hard reality. (It is no accident that candidates with a message of hope and optimism are more successful than candidates of gloom and doom.) In order to lead, presidents must juggle twenty different balls at once. It is no wonder that so few are up to the job.

Everybody Does It!

> A political leader must keep looking over his shoulder all the time to see if the boys are still there. If they aren't still there, he's no longer a political leader.
>
> —Bernard Baruch

In truth, presidents have always done polling. However, only in recent years have the more scientific and sophisticated forms of polling allowed presidents to get a precise and focused measure of the opinions of the public.

All good politicians take the pulse of the public. From Jackson's determination to use opinion as a club with which to beat the Congress into compliance, to Lincoln's "public baths" in the opinion of the moment, to FDR's sensitivity to the limits public opinion imposed on policy innovation, good politicians both use and are limited by opinion.[20]

It was during the presidency of Franklin Roosevelt that modern polling came into its own. Roosevelt took advantage of this new "scientific" polling to see how far he could go without getting too far ahead of the people. Harry Truman, his successor, was distrustful of polling and downright cynical about politicians whom he saw as slaves to opinion. Likewise, Dwight Eisenhower, while paying some attention to poll data, generally maintained a skeptical attitude towards their accuracy and utility.

It was during the presidencies of John Kennedy and Lyndon Johnson that polling moved squarely into the White House. From this point on, survey research became a part of daily White House operation. Richard Nixon took poll use up a notch. Lyndon Johnson commissioned 130 polls from 1963 to 1968; Nixon commissioned 233 during his first term! Nixon was obsessed with polls, and pollster Robert Teeter became an influential advisor, a role he would expand under President Ford.

Jimmy Carter took the next step, giving his in-house pollster, Pat Caddell, an office in the White House. And Ronald Reagan gave his pollster, Richard Wirthlin, amazing access to the president.[21] George Bush continued the trend, bringing Bob Teeter back into the presidential fold.

And so, when William Jefferson Clinton arrived at the White House, polling was deeply imbedded in the fabric of presidential politicking. If Bill Clinton kept reinventing himself, part of the reason for his many rebirths came from extensive use of survey research data. Clinton, like Nixon and Reagan before him, was obsessed with polls and used them extensively. Clinton went so far as to consult with pollsters and political strategists prior to choosing his summer vacation spot! Ironically, for a president obsessed with polls, Clinton took a surprisingly large number of stands that sharply differed from the public's.

The Use—and Misuse—of Polls

> Nothing is more dangerous than to live in the temperamental atmosphere of a Gallup poll, always taking one's pulse and taking one's temperature. . . . There is only one duty, only one safe course, and that is to try to be right and not to fear to do or say what you believe to be right.
>
> —Winston Churchill

That politicians use polls should not surprise us. But how they use polls can raise concern in a democratic republic. Do pollsters and consultants instruct presidents in how to give the public what it wants, and likewise, do presidents try to pander to the public? In short, is government a form of crass consumerism? Or do presidents *use* poll data to discern better ways to reach out to educate, and thereby lead the public?

Henry Kissinger noted that a statesman bridges the gap between vision and the nation's experiences. But can we expect mere politicians to rise to the level of statesman? Politicians, in order to stay in power, must sustain public support. Is it then any wonder that politicians rarely feel they can flaunt public opinion?

Leadership is about taking the public pulse and moving them, through vision and persuasion, in a desired direction. Leaders use polls to find out where the voters stand, and then—as FDR did prior to and during World War II—use that knowledge to educate, coax, nudge, push, pull, and "lead." Leaders know where they want to go and use polls to help them get the public behind their ideas.

Clinton advisor Dick Morris noted that

> Political opportunists won't do anything that is unpopular. Idealists will do unpopular things, but they almost insist on

> martyrdom. Pragmatists know they often have to embrace positions that the public doesn't like, but they work hard at articulating their views so as to survive to fight another day.[22]

Morris goes on to say:

> An idealistic leader will not hesitate to do something that is unpopular. But a smart idealist will carefully measure public opinion before he does so and will develop a strategy to persuade the electorate. Our sophisticated American electorate will come around if a leader takes the time to understand the concerns of his voters and addresses them articulately and well. In this way, polling makes strong leadership possible.[23]

If politics is the art of the possible, smart leaders go as far as they can, and push as much as is feasible, but know the limits of action. Leadership is about leading, not following. But leadership does not occur in a vacuum.

In a democracy, elected officials have a responsibility to and for the people. Their responsibility to the people is to faithfully represent them, to follow their direction, to serve their will. But a president's responsibility for the public revolves around efforts to lead in desired directions, to educate them in where they need to go, to supply motivation and direction. At the heart of the democratic leadership dilemma is the uneasy tension between following and leading.

And so, presidents can attempt to be *pied pipers*, leading an otherwise reluctant public; *puppets,* who slavishly follow the public mood; *persuaders,* who attempt to influence and convince the public; *panderers,* who play up to the weaknesses of the public; or *statesmen,* who ignore the public will and attempt a reflective form of rulership.

Actually, effective presidents are—at different times—all of these things. Effective leaders "style flex," that is, they fit their dance to the music being played. Since leadership is almost wholly contextual, effective leaders read the situation and fit their style to the context. Yes, politicians pander . . . sometimes. And they lead . . . sometimes. And they follow . . . sometimes.

With the proliferation of polling, presidents are more aware than ever of the views of the public, and they are evaluated by the public every day. It should come as no surprise that they are sensitive to the vagaries of public opinion. They must be.

Conclusion

> Those political leaders who shirk the task of popular education are misfits who do not understand the responsibilities of their jobs. And those leaders who act as if they thought the people to be fools responsive only to the meanest appeals deserve only scorn.
>
> —V. O. Key Jr.

Are the cynics correct? No. Actually, presidents pander much less often than the general public thinks.[24] The proliferation of polling gives the appearance that politicians pander, but the reality is that more often than not, they use polls to help them craft a message or move the public in a desired direction. Polls are more often tools of leadership than chains of slavery. We have less pandering than the public thinks, less leadership than the public needs, less political courage than democracy requires, more polls than are necessary, higher demands and expectations than a president can meet; and we grant less power than a president needs.

Notes

1. Cronin, "Leadership and Democracy," p. 36.
2. Bryce, *American Commonwealth*, p. 460.
3. Miroff, *Icons of Democracy*, p. 1.
4. Schlesinger Jr., *Cycles of American History*, p. 430.
5. Lincoln, "The Gettysburg Address." (ed. Cuomo and Holzer).
6. Randall, *Thomas Jefferson*. See also, Peterson, *Portable Thomas Jefferson*.
7. Miroff, *Icons of Democracy*, p. 354.
8. See Remini, *Andrew Jackson;* and Schlesinger Jr., *Age of Jackson*.
9. Genovese, *Power of the American Presidency*.
10. Morris, *New Prince*, p. 71.
11. Ibid., pp. 71–72.
12. Ibid., p. 75.
13. Genovese, *Presidential Dilemma*.
14. Zeidenstein, "Presidents' Popularity and Their Wins and Losses."

15. Brody, *Assessing the President.*

16. Ibid.

17. Summaries of the literature on the impact of the economy can be found in Kernell, *Going Public*, chap. 7; and Edwards, *Public Presidency*, chap. 6..

18. Brace and Hinckley, *Follow the Leader,* p. 45.

19. Hart, *Sound of Leadership.*

20. Genovese, *Power of the American Presidency.*

21. Beal and Hinckley, "Presidential Decision Making and Public Opinion Polls."

22. Morris, *New Prince*, p. 83.

23. Ibid., p. 84.

24. Jacobs and Shapiro, *Politicians Don't Pander.*

3

Presidential Leadership and the Threat to Popular Sovereignty

Lawrence R. Jacobs
and
Melinda S. Jackson

> The issues a candidate chooses to talk about . . . give people insight into just what kind of a person that candidate is.
>
> —Robert Teeter, President Bush's 1992 campaign manager and pollster for Richard Nixon

> [Governor Bush's] proposals may seem small, but aides say Mr. Bush is using the ideas to shape his image. [A] Bush adviser said, "Issues are important as reflections of values and keys into a candidate's leadership." He said independent swing voters "are not taking their stands on individual issues, but their feelings about what values the candidate reflects."
>
> —*New York Times*, 17 July 2000.

Competitive elections are a defining characteristic of representative democracies. Competitive and inclusive elections have long been heralded as establishing an institutional avenue for holding government officials accountable to the citizenry and, specifically, for exerting pressure on politicians to be responsive to the hard, substantive policy preferences of citizens. According to enduring political science theories,

---

We acknowledge the superior research assistance of Eric Ostermeier, Melanie Burns, and Brandon Thompson.

the inclination of voters to choose candidates with policy positions closest to their own generates powerful incentives for candidates to adopt positions that are favored by majorities or large groups of voters.[1] When majorities favor abortion under certain circumstances, extending health insurance to women and children, or ending military engagements, candidates are expected to elbow each other out of the way to be the first to embrace these positions as their own. Hand-to-hand combat to win elections is expected to give life to the revered principle of popular sovereignty; the result is that the policy preferences of the majority drive the behavior of candidates as well as presidents and legislators who are intent on winning elections for themselves and their political party.

Candidates and officeholders seeking election are not, however, simply auctioneers raffling off their policy positions to the largest number of voters. The hope that competitive elections will hold politicians accountable and transform them into eager followers of the policy preferences of citizens has crumbled as we have learned more about elections. Voters lack the time and don't make the effort to gather information about which government policies they most prefer or to sort out candidates and government officials who come closest to their views. Put simply, there is more to life today than politics.[2] In addition, candidates and officeholders are beholden to activists within political parties as their "core" group of supporters; candidates rely on activists' time, money, and votes in the primaries and general election.[3] This critical group of party activists often holds policy preferences far different from those of a majority of voters—think of the strong views of core Republicans about prohibiting abortion or those of die-hard Democrats about government health insurance for the entire population. The bottom line is that politicians are under heavy pressure to adopt policy positions preferred by party activists and, if necessary, to discount or dodge the policy positions preferred by the majority of voters.[4]

The policy stands of candidates and elected officials are often driven by party activists and are beyond the concern of most voters. How, you wonder, do voters reach decisions about which politicians to elect? The answer is that most voters handle the complex tasks of acquiring and processing information on policy issues by falling back on less taxing cognitive strategies—namely, by summarizing specific information about the candidates in general judgments about their personality attributes or, put most simply, image. Instead of policy issues driving voters, research now suggests that the electorate relies on personality, character, and personal image.[5]

There is a critical missing link in this story: the calculated strategy of politicians. It makes logical and practical sense that ambitious politicians would appeal to voters on the basis of their personal image rather than by hard, substantive policies: projecting an appealing image offers a way to hold the loyalty of the party activists (who could revolt against compromises of intensely supported policies) while attracting wavering voters who are swayed by an appealing personality.

We know very little, though, about the strategies of campaigns to manipulate candidate image. How have politicians crafted their public statements, messages, and presentations as part of calculated efforts to influence voters' evaluations? This chapter focuses on the strategies of presidents and, in particular, on the extensive private polling of Richard Nixon's White House. Did Nixon's steady stream of polls equip him to manipulate the public's perception of his image or personality attributes to distract voters from his unpopular policies while still winning elections? Even when Nixon focused on policy, how did he use his position on issues to affect the public's perceptions of his character and image? Finally, what are the implications for the strategy of image making for representative democracy and the principle of accountability? This chapter addresses these questions by examining the White House's memoranda, its write-ups of surveys, and the voluminous diary of Nixon's chief of staff (H. R. Haldeman).

Welcome to the Nixon Research Center

Many students of election campaigns assume that politicians suffer from incomplete information and act with great trepidation because of their anxiety over what they do not know about the electorate. The reality is that presidents, beginning in earnest with John Kennedy, have conducted extensive polling; few have conducted as much polling and made as many innovations in political polling as Richard Nixon's White House.[6] The Nixon White House continuously commissioned comprehensive public opinion surveys and certainly was not constrained by uncertainty regarding voters' attitudes; in fact, the opposite pattern existed: Nixon and his aides received a steady supply of new information and were confident in it and in their capacity to generate whatever information about voters might be lacking. Far from constraining its political and campaign strategy, the White House's information on voters boosted its confidence in identifying voters' attitudes and in attempting to manipulate the public's image of Nixon.

Poll 'til You Drop

Although presidents over the past four decades have collected the surveys that were published in newspapers and broadcast on television and radio, John Kennedy, Lyndon Johnson, and Nixon all preferred their own private polls. Private surveys gave presidents control over the distribution of polling results; they reasoned that possessing secret information that was denied other politicians (in an era of limited polling) provided them with a critical advantage in anticipating future public reactions.

Nixon relied on a stable of trustworthy Republican pollsters to conduct his research; the national Republican Party generally paid the pollsters, though Nixon did use a private stash of funds to pay for special surveys.[7] Nixon believed that keeping his polling results confidential maximized the "power in having the statistics yourself."[8] In addition, Nixon preferred his private surveys because they were more in-depth than the published surveys. Indeed, Nixon's demand for private polling was driven by his repeated frustration with being forced to "almost exclusively rely on Gallup or Harris."[9]

The number of private polls conducted for the White House rose dramatically between Kennedy's 1960 presidential campaign and Johnson's and Nixon's terms as president. In Kennedy's campaign to win the 1960 Democratic nomination he commissioned Louis Harris to conduct 50 polls during the Democratic primary contests and an additional 27 during the general election. Once in office, the administration received 16 private polling reports prepared by Harris.[10] Lyndon Johnson relied on Oliver Quayle, who provided 130 surveys; 39 surveys were conducted prior to the 1964 election, 30 were sent to the White House during 1965, 49 during 1966, 3 in 1967, and 9 in 1968.[11]

Nixon dramatically escalated the sheer number of private surveys. During his first term in office, the number of private surveys ballooned to 233, with 7 conducted during 1969, 29 in 1970, 44 in 1971, and 153 in 1972. In addition to conducting more surveys than President Kennedy (by a factor of over ten) and Johnson (by nearly a factor of two), the scope and content of Nixon's surveys were far more extensive and sophisticated.

The Polling Never Stops

The significant amount of polling in 1972 should not obscure an important development during the Nixon presidency—information on public attitudes was collected well before the 1972 election. More than his predecessors, Nixon extended the use of polling to the governing process. The number of polls conducted during nonelection years rose dramatically under Nixon; it was fivefold greater than during the Kennedy years. (Nixon conducted about as many surveys outside of the presidential election year as Johnson, though—as suggested below—they were far more substantial in their size and scope.) Nixon accepted the argument that regular polling should become a "permanent concern to the White House, rather than just [used] during elections."[12]

Three factors prompted Nixon and his aides to extend polling from election to nonelection periods. First, they valued precision, and social science methodology offered them a new kind of reliable and exact information and analysis. The White House's research on personality attributes was heavily influenced by survey research; White House aides and consultants drew on publications in the field's leading journal, *Public Opinion Quarterly*, which sparked (among other developments) the tracking of semantic differentials.[13] White House pollsters like Robert Teeter, who recruited survey methodologists like Fred Steeper (who was trained at the University of Michigan's Institute for Social Research) incorporated new statistical and measurement techniques into their research. For the first time, the White House received multivariate statistical analyses of survey data.[14]

The allure of social science should not be overstated. The practical and pressing concerns of Nixon and his aides made them impatient and frustrated with what social science could deliver. For instance, in the heat of the 1972 fall campaign, Nixon lashed out at the White House surveys, declaring that "Teeter's polling is a disaster" because his research focused on "our old constituency in the fashionable suburbs instead of the Colson hardhats and blue collar types. . . . [and has] ignored . . . the military, amnesty, [and] bussing."[15]

Second, White House aides and, indeed, Nixon himself consistently emphasized the importance of developing trend items—identically worded questions that would detect changes in public attitudes. Determining whether the public's approval level of Nixon's performance in office, its preferences for policies, and its evaluations of his personal traits were better or worse required having baseline data and monitoring variations. Prior to 1972 Nixon instructed his pollsters to ask specific questions in order to develop trend lines that could be used later during the election.

The third and perhaps most significant reason for continuously tracking public opinion was that the Nixon team recognized that "first impressions" count and are hard to dislodge once they are allowed to form. Waiting until 1972 to track and attempt to change public attitudes would be too late to be effective in influencing the election's outcome. Fending off negative perceptions was part of why the White House conducted and used polling early in his first term. The Nixon team also hoped to build public support for later use: it was critical to create an "aura" and "mystique" around Nixon to guarantee support in times of crisis.[16]

In the Nixon group's view, then, winning in 1972 meant that protecting and enhancing the president's standing with the public should be an ever-present consideration. Detailed planning and analysis of survey research surveys occurred years before Election Day in 1972.[17]

What Nixon's Polls Contained

Nixon and his advisers primarily relied on the Opinion Research Commission and Market Opinion Research to collect information about three areas of public opinion. First, the White House meticulously tracked the public's ranking of Nixon as a president and candidate. It regularly measured the public's approval of the president's performance both overall and in handling specific areas of domestic and foreign policy—from unemployment, crime, drugs, and the environment to Vietnam and foreign policy.

The president's team also matched Nixon up against hypothetical and real Democratic and independent opponents beginning in May 1970 (two and a half years before Election Day).

It is hardly surprising that the White House regularly conducted trial heats to judge Nixon's standing with potential competitors; this is the most obvious reason to conduct surveys. What is surprising is the extent of White House research and analysis of public attitudes that were *not* related to public approval and trial heats. Nixon and his aides wanted to know not only the president's standing in voters' summary measures (job approval and candidate choice in trial heats) but also *why* the public had reached those evaluations and *how* they could be changed. Nixon's persistent questions to his pollsters and staff about why the public reached its ranking and how it could be changed fundamentally concerned strategy; the connection between available information about voters and campaign strategy was quite close. Answering Nixon's questions required extensive research and dominated most of his surveys. The two remaining areas of public opinion were geared to answering Nixon's demand for explanations of voters' summary evaluations.

The second aspect of public opinion that Nixon researched was the public's attitudes toward policy issues. The White House's surveys carefully tracked what the public ranked as the most important problems facing the country. The White House also conducted polling on public attitudes toward specific issues within three broad policy areas: foreign policy (Vietnam and national defense), economic policy (inflation, unemployment, taxes, and government spending), and domestic issues (student demonstrations, crime, law and order, drugs, health care, education, welfare, environment, poverty, race relations, and civil rights issues including bussing and desegregation). Finally, it investigated the public's perception of legislative affairs and, specifically, congressional handling of presidential proposals. The result was a massive collection of public opinion data on issues. (A nearly three-hundred-page binder is filled with the kind of public opinion trends that are currently published in *Public Opinion Quarterly*.)

Nixon's interest in responding to the public's policy preferences by changing his positions to move closer to the public's was constrained by the strong and intense views of the Republican Party core. Haldeman alerted Nixon that Patrick Buchanan had strongly criticized the administration for its "move to the left" and warned that "he doesn't want to get too far off of his natural base."[18]

The third area of public opinion tracked by the Nixon crew was personal attributes and image of the president and his rivals. Nixon's pollsters began asking about personality trait ratings in December 1969 and over the next three years used two different question formats. In one format, they solicited open-ended responses to questions such as "What is the first thing that comes to mind when you think of Richard Nixon?" This format was also used for Nixon's opponents.

The second and more consistently used format relied on paired semantic differentials, which asked respondents to rate Nixon and his rivals on a series of opposite adjectives (such as "Fair" and "Unfair" or "Bold" and "Timid") along a seven-point scale. The White House experimented with the number of traits and the specific descriptive adjectives. One of its most extensive studies of public opinion was an "Image Poll" in May 1971, which posed thirty-four paired differentials to cover dimensions ranging from leadership, reliability, and duty, to sensitivity and sociability. By December 1971, the polling team had narrowed down the list of semantic differentials to eighteen, which they used until June 1972. The White House categorized these eighteen trait items into four dimensions: competence, amiability, strength, and trust.[19]

Campaign Strategies in an Era of Extensive Information

The White House's information on the public's attitudes toward policy issues and personal image was used as a political tool for two purposes: diagnosis of political conditions and fashioning a political therapy to improve Nixon's position. The White House used its polling to dissect the public's overall evaluations in approval ratings and trial heats and to identify the relative influence of the public's perception of his image on these evaluations. For instance, Haldeman reported in December 1970 that Nixon "does want the personal idea of the President to come through. He uses the polls as a basis for concluding that none of it has."[20] Once the White House had diagnosed the president's political ailments, they used polling to fashion an effective political therapy. The changing political and electoral conditions from 1969 to 1972 affected the White House's research on public opinion and strategies to change it.

1969: Wake-up Call

The first six months after Nixon's inauguration delivered a wake up call to the president and his aides. The political problems they confronted with Vietnam and domestic issues produced growing concerns about how Americans perceived the administration. The White House commissioned seven polls on the president's popularity and attitudes toward issues; in December they explored for the first time the public's ratings of personality traits. All of these were national surveys.

By the fall, Nixon and his chief of staff (Haldeman) were increasingly discussing the need to protect the president's position by engaging in aggressive efforts to shape public opinion. According to Haldeman's exhaustive (and remarkably candid) notes on his meetings with the president and other senior aides, Nixon requested that Haldeman form a White House group that would launch an "overall game plan and presidential offensive project, specifically on the President's image."[21]

1970: Nixon's Nervous Nellies

Political nervousness swept through the upper ranks of the White House in 1970. In an usual display of anguish and direct confrontation, senior officials confronted Haldeman in a staff meeting about the president's "loss of momentum and leadership in public eyes." This "substantial problem," Haldeman reports, was pinned on Nixon's conduct: John Ehrlichman, Bryce Harlow, Ron Ziegler, and Herbert Klein all concluded that the "President's theories of isolation and remoteness are badly aggravating [his problems]." While the staff blamed Nixon, the president blamed his staff.[22] As opposition grew to the president and his policies during the year, Nixon increasingly devoted his meetings with Haldeman to "long analysis of PR and where we've failed."[23] Election Day in 1972 was nearly three years off, but Nixon feared that he was squandering a critical time to "move fast and hard now to build up mystique. . . . [and] equity now on the personal side so when the attacks come the person stays above the attack."[24] The battle over setting first impressions was not going well.

DIAGNOSING NIXON. Nixon and his advisers requested an increasing number of polls to diagnose why voters were turning against the president. The White House possessed sixty-five substantial surveys in 1970, twenty-nine of which were conducted by its stable of pollsters, with the surveys split evenly between national samples and samples within specific states.[25]

For Nixon, the problem lay in his image. "The President's main thrust," Haldeman reported in January 1970, "is that we haven't adequately developed the image of him and his role and the office."[26] As his approval ratings fell from over 60% in 1969 to just above 50% over the course of 1970, White House research focused on dissecting these summary measures of Nixon for clues as to why the public was turning against him—what factors does the "president's approval and disapproval rating . . . stem [from]"?

The White House's polling consultant (David Derge, a political science professor at Indiana University who specialized in survey research) concluded from sorting through verbatim responses to survey questions that the public's perception of the president's general image was more important than reactions to specific issues: "[A] majority of the people will judge the President on his general performance, his approach to his duties, and his style in office," "with no mention of specific policies or events." Vietnam and the condition of the economy were identified as the two significant policy issues in the public's view, with other issues affecting only a "small part of the President's approval and disapproval rating."[27] A top Haldeman lieutenant instructed Derge later in the year about "the areas that should be probed and tested" with "regard to image" and reported back to commander Haldeman that Derge would immediately submit "final proposed quests for the image poll. . . . [that] will include those items mentioned in the President's recent memo to you on image."[28]

Nixon and his aides concluded from their information on public opinion that the failure to "creat[e] or conve[y] [the] idea of mystique" and "aura" has meant that "the President's support in the country is quite thin and shallow," with supporters (like hard-hat construction workers in New York City) "marching for him because they were against his opponents rather than because they were for him." Nixon and his staff complained that in "getting across to the public the idea that the president and his administration [operate]. . . . as an efficient, cold, machine," "[w]e have failed to convey any sense of human, warm, or personal charm associated with the President." Not only did the administration convey Nixon as machine-like, they "failed to get across. . . . areas of decency and virtues which the great majority of Americans like," such as "hard work, warmth, kindness, consideration of others, willingness to take the heat and not pass the buck, just plain guts and courage, [boldness], [and]. . . . do[ing] what he thinks is right regardless of the consequences."[29] Although Haldeman was Nixon's obedient soldier, Nixon's obsessive and "long harangue[s] about his revised views on PR" drove Haldeman to confide that he wished "[Nixon] would quit worrying about it and just be President."[30]

The diagnosis was clear: Nixon needed to convey a new image of himself to Americans.

GOING FOR IMAGE. The remedy to the president's fragile public support, he and his aides believed, lay in getting the "personal idea of the President to come through" by improving the performance of the administration's public relations machine (not in changing the message). "We've totally failed," Nixon informed Haldeman, "in our real PR."[31] The "whole thrust," senior officials told Haldeman, "is on the need for appearance, not substance"[32] and (Nixon emphasized) "get[ting] across what kind of a man the President is"—his "boldness, guts, etc., rather than how well the machinery works."[33]

Despite his pique at Americans' perceptions, Nixon's first instinct was to improve the machine. If the administration's public relations apparatus performed better in "getting out the line about decisiveness, command, etc.," he would get "credit for it" and the public would feel better about him as a person. In particular, Nixon was convinced that the fix was in creating "better press on the President's image and leadership" by redirecting the administration's backgrounders for journalists toward the "personality of the man."[34] Using the backgrounders to "get through" the themes of a "hard-working," "courageous," "strong," intelligent" president "is a challenge that we should not let go unanswered."[35] In addition, Nixon expected his speeches to be used more effectively to "get across the leadership image. . . . to bypass the media and get directly to the people."[36] Finally, the White House displayed Nixon himself more often. The purpose of "more public presidential presentations, press conferences, speeches, [and] review trips," Nixon and his senior aides agreed, "[is] [n]ot so much to sell programs but to demonstrate that the President cares."[37]

DEMONSTRATING NIXON "THE MAN". In addition to improving the performance of the administration's public relations apparatus, to boost his image Nixon headquarters designed a strategy of highlighting policy decisions that were supported and respected by the public. Nixon instructed Haldeman that three of his "major accomplishments: Cambodia, the Middle East, and the Vietnam Speech. . . . [should be used to] get across the courage, the independence, [and] the boldness . . . of the President . . . ."[38] "If we had gotten across, for example, the Cambodian decision making adequately," then the public should have viewed the president as courageous.[39] Nixon and his aides also planned to use his decision to overrule the "Cabinet on [proposing a] Family Assistance [program]" to "get across" the president's "boldness" and "courage" in "stepping up to a hard one and hitting it."[40]

Gearing up for the Election: 1971

Nixon began 1971 on an expansive note; he alerts Haldeman that he "wants to use this year to fill the canvass. . . . [and use the media] to hit all the leadership and image things that we feel we need to do."[41]

Nixon's hopes were soon jarred, however. In January, he was "bothered" by approval ratings in the Gallup Organization's most recent poll that were 6 percentage points lower than his private results.[42] By February, he began to accept that his approval ratings were "not very good" and worried that his "image is set now and there's nothing we can do to change it."[43] In the summer, approval ratings dropped below the critical threshold of 50%, and the White House's "Image Poll" revealed to Nixon and his senior aides "very clear weak points."[44] Haldeman, who was closely involved with the Image Poll, conducted a "long review" with Nixon, who was "obviously and justifiably concerned" by the failure of "personal characteristic[s]" to get through to Americans.[45]

Nixon's souring political fortunes created a new sense of urgency, with the president ordering "a shift . . . throughout our entire shop to begin a totally oriented commitment to relating everything we do to the political side . . . [and constantly asking,] Does this help us politically?"[46]

Picking up on his complaints during 1970, Nixon pinned his sliding public standing on "lousy" public relations that "lack[ed] . . . focus and intelligence."[47]

DIAGNOSING NIXON. Nixon and his advisers increasingly turned to polls for information on public opinion that would pinpoint why Americans were not embracing the president. Their supply of private surveys sharply rose from twenty-nine in 1970 to forty-four, with three times as many polls based on national samples as state samples.[48] As information on public opinion became more ample and influential on White House strategy, the demand for a deeper insight into public attitudes rose. "We would like to find out," Haldeman's assistant said to his polling coordinator, "what people feel is positive about this Administration" as well as the public's reservations and dislikes.[49] A persistent theme among White House officials was the complaint that "our program could be more intelligently directed" if they could "ascertain what . . . qualities are . . . [most] important [in influencing presidential approval]."[50]

The White House's growing reliance on polling information to pinpoint the factors in the public's summary evaluations of Nixon was reflected not only in the widening use of Nixon's stable of pollsters but also in the planning for an unprecedented level of polling during 1972. Almost a year and a half from the elections, Nixon's campaign was preparing to stock its offices with ample information on public opinion; it reported that "considerable attention is currently being devoted to planning for polling in the 1972 campaign," including "detailed operating plans," the selection of pollsters, and the formulation of research designs.[51]

Implementation of Nixon's insistence on "relating everything we do to the political side" was evident in the selection of polling sites based on the electoral college[52] and in the designing of a finely honed strategy to "identif[y] and communicat[e] with the ambivalent voter" through "direct mail, precinct work [and other methods]."[53] As Nixon's approval ratings sagged, he and his aides concentrated on using their survey information, particularly from their "Image and Issue Studies," to dissect these summary measures. The objective was to understand the voters with "polling [used to] bring out [their] current attitudes on the issues and the candidates."[54]

Nixon and his senior aides renewed and deepened their commitment to using polling for two purposes. First, they demanded information on voters' attitudes toward policy and "whether our position [on specific issues] has gone up or down in the eyes of the public."[55]

The second attraction of survey research to Nixon and his senior aides was that it investigated public perceptions of the personality traits of the major candidates. As one aide emphasized to the chief of staff, many of the "major reasons for approving of [the president's] performance . . . were really not judgments on substantive issues or accomplishment, but were subjective judgments about the man."[56] Tracking Nixon's image became more important in light of continuing evidence on "presidential personality standings. . . . [that] showed he had declined in the rating of strength and decisiveness, the two characteristics [Nixon] feels are most important for [the administration] to get over."[57] In addition to investigating the "image of . . . an ideal president" and the image of the Nixon administration, the White House was especially focused on surveying how people thought about Nixon and why.[58]

As a result of this intense demand for more information on the public's evaluation of Nixon's personality traits, the White House conducted an "Image Poll" that included—under the strict direction of Haldeman and his staff—a closely reviewed set of semantic differentials and major terms on which Nixon was rated. The purpose was to analyze the factors that influenced the public's broader summary evaluations, such as approval and candidate choice.[59]

THE POLITICAL THERAPY. The remedy to the president's fragile public support, Nixon instructed his chief of staff, lay in, first, "getting a clear, decisive picture before the voters with regard to the President as a man (leader, etc.) and, second, our three or four major issues as far as political clout is concerned."[60] Two facets of Nixon's strategy are especially significant. First, rather than treating issues and image as mutually exclusive, Nixon and his senior aides repeatedly singled out polls showing that the two were both critical to their success. As one aide explained, "[P]olling brings out [voters'] current attitudes on the issues and candidates . . . [that] provide a solid basis for strategic and tactical campaign decisions."[61] The president instructed Haldeman to consult senior "PR types" to "get some agreement as to what points [about issues and image] we want to hammer home . . . and agree upon for emphasis for the balance of this year."[62] Nixon and his aides concentrated more than in 1970 on the content of the message itself and on issues to be repeated and traits to be emphasized."[63]

Second, Nixon insisted in 1971 on avoiding ambiguity in favor of following clear directions that set him off from rivals. "We've got to quit zigzagging and establish a cutting edge" in a "very hard direction" on "one or two things . . . [that are] in front of us at all times." Nixon's fear was that trying to build a consensus made him look indecisive[64]

Nixon insisted that the way to fix his weak standing with Americans was a clear, coordinated message. He assigned Haldeman the job of identifying the administration's message and how it should be implemented.[65] The White House's polls on issues and image were utilized to guide "advertising people [who will] settle on themes," decisions on scheduling, press conferences, and television appearances by the president.[66] Nixon committed himself to using the "enormous" "power of the office . . . [for] showmanship. . . . [and] the appearance of action" in a way that "commands the news, [demonstrates] leadership, and knocks everyone else out of the news." The "effective use of TV. . . . [would] get through the symbolism of contact with a lot of people" in a way that would "dominate the dialogue" and "get that appearance of leadership."[67]

One vehicle for conveying clear and distinct policy positions and images to Americans was an improved public relations apparatus. Appointing a "full-time PR man" was Nixon's proposed fix for the problem of having "no system . . . of getting [telling incidents of the president's personality] to public attention."[68] Nixon also instructed Haldeman to have the staff stress the president's leadership qualities.[69] Haldeman then ordered senior officials (like current *New York Times* columnist William Safire) who were responsible for public relations to "integrate [the themes of a hardworking, dignified, courageous, and strong leader] into an overall plan on press relations."[70]

Nixon and his aides pursued two strategies in tailoring his messages to highlight poll-identified issues and personality traits: one aimed to boost his image and the other his policy stances.

MANAGING NIXON'S IMAGE. Nixon and Haldeman remained consistently focused on "the job we're to do in the personality side"[71] and, as an aide put it, on projecting the "important qualities of . . . leadership and . . . car[ing]."[72] For Nixon, image was every bit as important as policy issues in reaching Americans: he directed Haldeman to "concentrate on. . . . the basic point of leadership: boldness, courage, etc. . . . [and] the personal family man [with] character, decency" along with achievements in foreign policy and in creating "prosperity without war and without inflation."[73]

The administration promoted Nixon's image by hyping favorably perceived traits and minimizing unpopular aspects of the president's personality. The White House's outside polling experts recommended that its "strategy should stress the administration's achievements and presidential roles and characteristics already seen in a favorable light" and "not try to remake the President's image." In particular, they proposed emphasizing Nixon's positive personality traits, such as being courageous, concerned about people, experienced, self-confident, cautious, dignified, active, strong, hardworking, dedicated, and possessing high ideals. To promote Nixon's personality strengths, advisors recommended a series of trips and television productions.[74] In addition, Nixon proposed that Haldeman "have people like Kissinger, Moynihan, Ehrlichman, and others . . . search their memories as well as their files and records to . . . come up with . . . actions by the President which reflect the man rather than his process or policies" and "convey the true image of a President."[75]

The Nixon group also attempted to promote some of the president's underappreciated personality traits by highlighting popular policies.[76] Nixon emphasized the impact of his trip to China on his leadership image because it changed public perceptions and made him "appear bold." The trip was expected to give "all the other things we do . . . a different flavor" by, for instance, getting "people to play back to the China thing in the dialogue on the economy because the main point in both cases is leadership."[77] Nixon's initiative on Cambodia in November 1970 also offered an opportunity to portray the president as an independent leader.[78]

The general strategy, one aide suggested, is to have the administration's spokesmen stress Nixon's presidential leadership and to give more "exposure" to proposals that reflect Nixon's positive personality traits. Advisors recommended framing State of the Union proposals to reflect "that the President cares deeply about the poor and the sick and the disadvantaged."[79]

Nixon headquarters was mostly concerned in 1971 with the fact that his "story is not being heard by the people." The result is that "aside from withdrawing from Vietnam no other positive action by the Nixon administration stands out [and] . . . [m]ore than a third of the public are unable to cite anything the administration has accomplished."[80] And being associated with Vietnam was dangerous. One of the White House's pollsters warned that "Vietnam is at core of all problems."[81]

Nixon was understandably distressed that nearly three years into his term, the administration's message was still not clear to the public. His orders to his most trusted aides were to "create issues" by "pick[ing] out three issues that really matter. . . . [even] if it is [not] something we will actually accomplish." The key point, Nixon emphasized, was to avoid ambiguity: he demanded "issues that will give us sharp image. . . . [and put us] on [one] side or the other. We can't be neither."[82] He emphasized—with support from his polls—that drugs and crime in general were the "only issue[s] we can gain very much from emphasizing"; they were accomplishments that had not been "appreciated" and would benefit from being "dramatized."[85] The White House's challenge was to "personally identif[y]" Nixon with issues of importance to Americans.[84]

The Election of 1972

Richard Nixon beat George McGovern in an electoral college landslide. But during 1972, the Nixon crew was anxious. In the spring, Nixon and Haldeman were alerted that state-level polls indicated that "it is important for the President to improve his standing in several crucial states during the next few weeks [where] . . . there is a substantial number of undecided voters who can be turned into committed Nixon voters if given some attention before the actual campaign period begins."[85] Haldeman reported in early October that Nixon's popularity suffered "some erosion" and was "not too good" as it fell nine points and McGovern's rose three.[86]

The approach of Election Day intensified the interest of the White House and the campaign staff in trial heat surveys and in public opinion research on issues and image. In response to the demand, Nixon and his advisers were literally inundated by an unprecedented avalanche of polls.

The White House commissioned 153 private surveys in 1972, three times the level in 1971 and more than either John Kennedy or Lyndon Johnson conducted during their entire terms: Nixon's polling in 1972 increased two and a half times over the number Kennedy assembled from 1958 to 1960 and was 80 percent greater than those commissioned by Johnson in the year before the 1964 election and during 1968. Nixon conducted more surveys in 1972 than Johnson's total for his *entire* presidency.

The intense focus of Nixon and his advisers on his relative standing and on ever more detailed information about voters drove the campaign's pollsters toward greater precision about voter attitudes on issues and personality traits to help develop campaign strategy. In addition to trial heats, these surveys tracked personality attributes, preferences toward issues, and the most important problems facing the country as well as the candidates' ranking in terms of their ability to handle them.

The unprecedented outpouring of detailed, state-level surveys guided the "strategic thrust [of] the campaign" in terms of its messages, travel, actions, and advertisements. They were also used to "pinpoint . . . areas where ticket-splitting is highest [in order to] allocate our resources there" and "give us our margin of victory."[87] State-of-the-art statistical methods were used to "identify the most important independent factors which influence the presidential vote"; this allowed the campaign to separate out the roles of partisanship, issue attitudes, and candidate image.[88]

DIAGNOSING NIXON. Nixon and his senior aides combed through the polls and their sophisticated analysis to determine the factors that were driving voting choices.[89] In a series of statistical analyses of priority states that were sent to Haldeman and senior campaign officials in the spring, Teeter identified the factors affecting why one voted for Nixon rather than for his rivals (beginning with Muskie). He concluded that party identification was the "single most important vote determining factor for president," followed by voters' perception of Muskie's trustworthiness; voters' income and age; and Nixon's perceived trustworthiness and strength.[90] Separate analyses of Nixon's pairing with Kennedy and his pairing with Wallace found that "different factors explained Nixon's vote." Issues played a greater role in the Kennedy pairing and less of role when Wallace was included. The common theme in Teeter's analyses was the dominating influence of partisanship as well as the important role of voter's perceptions of candidates' personalities and competence on issues."[91]

Teeter later reported that additional analyses showed that the "vote determining factors varies considerably from state to state" but that the most important factors were party, followed by trust in Nixon, comparative issue handling ability, the competence of the opponent, and then a set of demographic variables. Ideology exerted little influence on vote choice.[92]

Nixon's advisers emphasized his image as a critical factor in the election's outcome. Teeter's analysis "ranked the President's perceived personality variables according to their importance in affecting the vote," singling out the "personality variables... which characterize the President as informed, experienced, competent, and safe."[93] The next most important factors were identified as voters' perceptions of the president's trustworthiness (namely, honesty, open-mindedness, and justness) and his issue-handling ability. Perceptions of competence (i.e., experience, training, and informed) were less influential. The surveys also indicated, however, weaknesses; in particular, that Nixon was "not perceived as frank, warm, extroverted, relaxed, [or possessing a] sense of humor."[94] According to Teeter, the "general perception of how well the President handles issues . . . appears to be more important to voting than perception of his handling of any one or two issues."[95]

The combination of weaknesses in Nixon's personal appeal and his issue positions was troubling to his senior campaign advisers. In unusually blunt language, Teeter reported that the president "does not have any great personal appeal and will not be re-elected on the basis of personality or personal appeal." But, Teeter warned, "We would have trouble trying to fight the campaign on [a] series of specific issues," because the "general attitude in the country toward government and politics is very negative."[96]

POLITICAL THERAPY. The strategy of the Nixon campaign was to emphasize the president's strengths and solidify public perceptions in areas where Nixon perceived his record to be strong, but had not gotten his message through.[97] Part of this strategy entailed seizing on his positive personality traits. Nixon and his advisers attempted to capitalize on the public's perception of him as competent by, as one aide recommended, "remaining very presidential on a pedestal above the battle": "the best politics . . . [is] to be totally consumed by enormous issues of war and peace, the future of America, strengthening the economy."[98]

The campaign calculated that it could use the president's strong personality traits to offset his weakness on policy issues. "Each of the Democratic candidates is perceived . . . as being able to handle domestic problems . . . more effectively than the President," wrote a campaign advisor. Nixon "must trade on [his] strength" of being "perceived as . . . the most experienced, the best trained, most informed, the most competent. . . .and bring them to bear on the domestic issues."[99]

Teeter reached a similar conclusion: he warned that "it will be more difficult . . . to attract the ticket-splitter on the basis of specific issues" and, instead, recommended that Nixon utilize his advantage on perceived competence to "show how the President's policies and programs fit into a plan" and constitute a "set of well-articulated goals for the country."[100]

The president's aides also recommended taking advantage of McGovern's "greatest weakness . . . [which is] a lack of competence" and Nixon's "greatest advantage over him." This opportunity for Nixon was compounded by the controversy about McGovern's running mate's treatment for mental illness.[102] Put simply, "competence helps Nixon and hurts McGovern."[102]

Presidential Strategy and Representative Democracy

Voters rely on image to choose candidates. Recent research has suggested that these images are not simply "fluff" devoid of substantive content about government policy. Instead, it is suggested that voters are efficiently tallying their more substantive judgments into overall evaluations of a politician's image and character. For instance, President Gerald Ford's bewilderment over how to eat a tamale provided information about his commitment to Hispanic voters.[103]

This hopeful interpretation of voters' reliance on image to choose among candidates, however, ignores the sophisticated polling of presidents and other high-level politicians to manipulate voters' perceptions. The reality is that politicians—and especially presidents—have the resources to distract or "divert" voters from unpopular policy issues. The strategy of image making raises the question whether image serves as an effective heuristic for voters. At risk is the ability of voters to reliably uphold the principle of popular sovereignty and government responsiveness to the policy preferences of majorities.

The nature of elite strategy raises significant questions about our understanding of the American democratic process. In the classic view of representative democracy, informed voters make choices among divergent candidates. Much of the debate about the viability of democratic governance has focused on the capability of voters. Joseph Schumpeter, Giovanni Sartori, and others offer a stinging critique of citizens as myopic and misinformed.[104] Alarmed about basing government on citizens, they narrow the definition of democracy to merely a "method" for selecting among competing sets of leaders, with citizens restricted to the role of "deciding the deciders" and discouraged from lobbying policymakers or in other ways interfering with their judgments. The overriding assumption is that expert answers to most government policies exist and that government officials (and other economic and political elites) monopolize that information as well as the wisdom about how best to use it. Put simply, this technocratic view of democracy claims that elites can be trusted to make the "right" decisions and voters need to stay out of the way.

One reaction of some political scientists has been to acknowledge the limited policy knowledge of citizens and instead to point to the crude retrospective judgments that they can reach based on everyday experiences—economic conditions, military conflict, and other circumstances that are readily observed in daily life. The busy voter reaches reasonable decisions concerning presidential candidates, according to this view, by simply deciding whether the economy and other conditions are better today than they were four years earlier. This retrospective model of representative democracy has grabbed the mantle of "realism" by accepting the limits of citizens while still maintaining that there is a reliable link between government officials and the real-world wants of voters.[105]

Evidence that presidents deploy sophisticated public opinion research to attempt to manipulate the perceptions and choices of citizens raises fundamental questions about the nature of representative democracy. Presidential efforts at manipulation pose a fundamental challenge to the technocratic view. The reality is that few, if any, significant government policy issues have objective "expert answers": Is there a "correct" way to extend health insurance or adequate food and housing to all Americans? Or are these goals and how we reach them thoroughly imbued with our beliefs about individual and community responsibility as well as our own assessments of risk? The lack of a definitive "correct" answer is particularly troubling today when government officials are ideologically polarized over the role of government—with liberals favoring a greater role and conservatives pushing for less. Research on congressional decision making shows that the two parties are further away from each other than at any time in the past century. Presidential attempts to manipulate voters in this context raise difficult questions. Is the health of our representative form of government most threatened by citizens struggling to balance a busy life with meaningful democratic participation or by elites intent on enacting the ideological agendas that they and their financial and party supporters favor? Put simply, are the strategies of political elites endangering the health of a vibrant representative democracy? Should we turn the spotlight from citizens and their flaws to the flaws of political elites? At the very least, the notion that government officials are neutral, competent technocrats requires more careful consideration.

Quite apart from the determined efforts of presidents to influence public evaluation is the critical question about the impact of these efforts. There may be determined efforts to manipulate public opinion, but voting based on whether the country is better today than four years ago may well still frustrate presidential efforts at manipulation. President Clinton, after all, attempted to create public support for his health care reform proposal by throwing the White House's resources into a "communications war."[106] However, the defeat of the Clinton health care plan may have represented an unusual confluence of interest group opposition, bipartisan unease, and public ambivalence.[107]

What is clear, though, is that presidents now have the capacity to launch laser-guided public relations campaigns to promote the policy that they and their backers most prefer. Any confidence in the technocratic expertise of policymakers or the potential for voters to cut through the hype to decipher meaningful information about the economy and other conditions is more difficult today. The new presidential capacity to track and attempt to alter public opinion poses troubling questions about the nature of American democracy.

Notes

1. This is often referred to as the "median voter theory" and is most closely associated with Anthony Downs (*Economic Theory of Democracy*; cf. Black, *Theory of Committees and Elections*). The theory focuses on the proximity or "closeness" of voters' preferred policy to those of the candidates.

2. Campbell et al., *American Voter*; Converse, "The Nature of Belief Systems"; Lau, "Political Motivation and Political Cognition"; Moskowitz and Stroh, "Expectation-Driven Assessments of Political Candidates"; Alvarez, *Information and Elections*.

3. Page, *Choice and Echoes*.

4. A number of studies in different western democracies have found that political parties and election candidates regularly adopt policy positions that are not responsive to the preferences of their electorates (Grofman, Griffin, and Glazer, "Identical Geography, Different Party"; Peltzman, "Constituent Interest and Congressional Voting"; Poole, "Dimensions of Interest Group Evaluation"; Poole and Rosenthal, "Patterns of Congressional Voting"; Rabinowitz, Macdonald, and Listhaug, "New Players in an Old Game"; Listhaug, Macdonald, and Rabinowitz, "A Comparative Spatial Analysis"; Dalton, "Political Parties and Political Representation"; Inglehart, "The Changing Structure of Political Cleavages"; Holmberg, "Political Representation in Sweden").

5. Markus and Converse, "A Dynamic Simultaneous Equation Model"; Miller, Wattenberg, and Malanchuk, "Schematic Assessments of Presidential Candidates"; Kinder and Sears, "Public Opinion and Political Action"; Lodge and Stroh, "Inside the Mental Voting Booth"; Wyer et al., "Image, Issues, and Ideology."

6. Jacobs, *Health of Nations*; Jacobs, "The Recoil Effect"; Jacobs, "Institutions and Culture"; Jacobs and Jackson, "Reconciling the Influence of Policy Issues"; Jacobs, Druckman, and Ostermeier, "A Political Theory of Candidate Strategy"; Jacobs and Shapiro, "The Rise of Presidential Polling."

7. Nixon's stable of pollsters was sizable. Opinion Research Corporation (ORC) and Chilton conducted most of Nixon's polling through 1971; Teeter primarily shared the work with Market Opinion Research (MOR) and Decision Making Information (DMI). Becker Research also conducted a small number of surveys. See Jacobs and Shapiro ("The Rise of Presidential Polling") for information on the funding of Nixon's research.

8. Interview with Dent by LRJ, 5/26/93.

9. HRH, Box 403, Memo to Haldeman from Higby, 4/7/70; HRH, Box 403, Memo to Haldeman from Nixon, 12/30/69; Haldeman Diaries (CD-Rom), 7/13/70 entry; HRH, Box 403, Memo to Haldeman from Nixon, 11/30/70.

10. JFK Library, POF, Boxes 104, 105, and 106; Jacobs and Shapiro, "Public Decisions, Private Polls"; Jacobs, "A Social Interpretation of Institutional Change"; Jacobs, "The Recoil Effect"; Jacobs, *Health of Nations*, pp. 138–44ff.; interview with Louis Harris by LRJ and RYS, 6/17/91.

11. In tabulating the number of private surveys done for the Johnson White House we focused on Quayle's surveys because they were most numerous, they were treated by the White House as "their" surveys (i.e., the findings were private and it used them to run its questions), and, finally, the connection to Quayle was rooted in a continuing relationship that began with Louis Harris's work for Kennedy. (When Harris became a public and publishing pollster, he curtailed his private polling for Kennedy and recommended Quayle as his replacement; Johnson continued Kennedy's relationship with Quayle [Jacobs, "A Social Interpretation of Institutional Change"].) Although Johnson primarily relied on Quayle (especially up to 1967), he did receive private polling data—as did Nixon—from the following sources: Louis, Bowles, and Grace (4); Belden; Political Surveys and Analysis; Central Surveys; Research Council (directed by Lloyd Free); Hamilton, Thomas, and Associates; International Research Week; Muchmore Polling (2); First Research Corporation (2); Opinion Research Associates (2); Cookerly; Delta; Indiana Democratic Committee; Kraft (11); and Napolitan (10). (The numbers in parentheses indicate the number of surveys forwarded to the White House; the names of some polling organizations were not indicated on their reports.) These surveys total 54 in all, but they were not treated with the same sustained interest as Quayle's polls; they were often sent unsolicited to the White House. LBJ Library, CF PR16, Box 80, 81, and 82; interview with Fred Panzer by LRJ, 11/12/92.

12. Interview with David Derge by LRJ, 5/17/93.

13. Of particular influence was a 1969 *Public Opinion Quarterly* article by David Berlo, James Lemert, and Robert Mertz. Public opinion survey, "Illinois Statewide I," December 1971. HRH, Box 381, p. 42.

14. Moore, *Superpollsters*, p. 223; Clymer, "A Bush Campaign Chief."

15. Haldeman Diary, entry for 10/10/72.

16. Memo to Derge from Higby, 12/28/70, HRH Box 403.

17. Haldeman Diaries (CD-Rom), 2/2/72 entry; HRH, Box 263, Memo to Haldeman from Derge, 11/27/70; HRH, Box 342, Memo to Haldeman from Higby, 12/9/70; HRH, Box 342, Memo to Higby from Strachan, 4/2/71; HRH, Box 342, Memo to Haldeman from Strachan, 4/3/71; HRH, Box 342, Memo to Mitchell from Magruder, 5/5/71; HRH, Box 349, "Ten Days after Victory: An Interim Report by the Committee for the Re-election of the President," 11/17/72.

18. Haldeman Diary, entry for 1/17/71.

19. The four dimensions closely parallel the three personality attributes identified by the existing research on voters' perceptions of candidate image,

with "amiability" capturing the "warmth" dimension used by scholars; Nixon's strength dimension was the one addition.

20. Haldeman Diary, entry for 12/3/70.

21. Haldeman Diary, entries for 8/25/69, 10/18/69, and 11/5/69.

22. Haldeman Diary, entry for 4/24/70.

23. Haldeman Diary, entry for 1/8/70.

24. Ibid.

25. The White House also retained surveys from a variety of sources, including state Republican parties and other politicians..

26. Haldeman Diary, entry for 1/8/70.

27. Memo to Nixon from Derge, 4/14/70, HRH Box 403.

28. Memo to Derge from Larry Higby, 12/28/70, HRH Box 403; Memo to Haldeman from Higby, 12/28/70, HRH, Box 403.

29. Memo to Derge from Higby, 12/28/70, HRH Box 403; Memo to Haldeman from Nixon, 12/1/70, PPF, Box 2..

30. Haldeman Diary, entry for 5/19/70.

31. Haldeman Diary, entry for 12/3/70.

32. Haldeman Diary, entry for 4/24/70.

33. Haldeman Diary, entry for 12/3/70.

34. Haldeman Diary, entry for 2/2/70.

35. Memo to Haldeman from Nixon, 12/1/70, PPF, Box 2; Memo to Derge from Higby, 12/28/70, HRH, Box 403.

36. Haldeman Diary, entry for 10/8/70.

37. Haldeman Diary, entry for 4/24/70.

38. Haldeman Diary, entry for 12/3/70.

39. Memo to Haldeman from Nixon, 12/1/70, PPF, Box 2.

40. Memo to Derge from Higby, 12/28/70, HRH Box 403.

41. Haldeman Diary, entry for 1/5/71.

42. Haldeman Diary, entry for 1/17/71.

43. Haldeman Diary, entry for 2/28/71.

44. Handwritten Notes: "Haldeman, L, Benham—Nixon Image Poll, 6/1" HRH, Box 334; White House surveys; Haldeman Diary, entry for 5/31/71.

45. Haldeman Diary, entries for 1/12/71 and 5/31/71.

46. Haldeman Diary, entries for 6/10/71 and 2/28/71.

47. Haldeman Diary, entries for 1/15/71 and 8/16/71.

48. Nearly all of the state samples were delivered after October.

49. Memo to Derge from Higby, 1/14/71, HRH Box 341.

50. Memo to Haldeman from Moore, 1/25/71, HRH Box 350, with Haldeman's handwritten note acknowledging that the recommended action was already in the works.

51. Memo to Mitchell from MacGruder and Higby, 6/8/71, HRH Box 263; Memo to Haldeman from Strachan, 10/6/71, HRH, Box 368; Memo to Haldeman from Benham, executive vice president of ORC, 5/5/71, HRH Box 334.

52. Memo to Mitchell from Teeter, 11/17/71, HRH Box 368; Memo to Haldeman from Teeter, 11/24/71, HRH, Box 368; "Tentative List of States to Be Polled," HRH Box 368.

53. Memo to Mitchell from Flanigan, 9/30/71; Memo to Mitchell and Haldeman from MacGruder and Higby, 6/23/71, HRH, Box 341.

54. Memo to Mitchell from Flanigan, 9/30/71, HRH Box 368; Memo to Haldeman from Benham, 5/5/71, HRH Box 334.

55. Memo to Derge from Higby, 1/14/71, HRH Box 341.

56. Memo to Haldeman from Moore, 1/25/71, HRH Box 350.

57. Haldeman Diary, entry for 2/15/71; Memo to Mitchell from Teeter, 11/17/71, HRH Box 368.

58. Memo to Derge from Higby, 1/14/71, HRH Box 341.

59. Memo to Derge from Higby, 1/14/71, HRH Box 341; Haldeman Diary, entry for 1/12/71.

60. Memo to Haldeman from Nixon, 6/28/71, PPF, Box 3.

61. Memo to Mitchell from Flanigan, 9/30/71, HRH Box 368.

62. Haldeman Diary, entry for 7/18/71.

63. Memo to Haldeman from Nixon, 6/28/71, PPF, Box 3; Haldeman Diary, entries for 1/5/71 and 4/14/71; Memo to Haldeman from Rumsfeld, 1/18/71, HRH, Box 350.

64. Haldeman Diary, entry for 6/10/71.

65. Haldeman Diary, entries for 1/15/71 and 4/3/71.

66. Memo to Mitchell from Teeter, 11/17/71, HRH, Box 368; Memo to Mitchell from Flanigan, 9/30/71, HRH Box 368.

67. Haldeman Diary, entries for 4/3/71, 8/16/71, and 9/17/71.

68. Memo to Haldeman from Nixon, 3/1/71, PPF, Box 3.

69. Haldeman Diary, entries for 6/26/71 and 1/17/71.

70. Memo to Safire from Haldeman, 1/18/71, HRH Box 350.

71. Haldeman Diary, entry for 2/15/71.

72. Memo to Haldeman from Moore, 1/25/71, HRH Box 350.

73. Haldeman Diary, entry for 8/16/71.

74. Memo to Haldeman from Strachan, 7/19/71 regarding Derge Analysis of Nixon Image Study, HRH Box 343; Memo to Haldeman from Bentham, 5/9/71, HRH Box 343; Memo to Nixon from Derge, 7/4/71, HRH Box 343.

75. Memo to Haldeman from Nixon, 3/1/71, PPF, Box 3.

76. Memo to Nixon from Derge, 7/4/71, HRH Box 343.

77. Haldeman Diary, entries for 7/18/71 and 8/16/71.

78. Haldeman Diary, entry for 1/15/71; Memo to Haldeman from Moore, 1/25/71, HRH Box 350.

79. Memo to Haldeman from Moore, 1/25/71, HRH Box 350.

80. Memo to Nixon from Derge, 7/4/71, HRH Box 343.

81. Handwritten Notes: "Haldeman, L, Benham—Nixon Image Poll, 6/1," HRH, Box 334; White House surveys; Haldeman Diary, entry for 5/31/71.

82. Haldeman Diary, entry for 6/9/71.

83. Haldeman Diary, entry for 5/31/71; Memo to Nixon from Derge, 7/4/71, HRH Box 343.

84. Memo to Haldeman from Benham, 6/9/71, HRH 343.

85. Memo to Mitchell from Teeter, 3/3/72, HRH Box 362.

86. Haldeman Diary, entry for 10/2/72.

87. Memo to Nixon from Teeter, 3/3/72; HRH Box 362; "Position Paper: The 1972 Campaign, 4/18/72," HRH Box 358; HRH Box 363, Memo to Chapin from Teeter, 7/25/72 (marked "Confidential"); HRH Box 362, Memo to Mitchell from Teeter, 5/11/72.

88. Memo to Mitchell from Teeter, 5/11/72, HRH Box 362; Memo to Chapin from Teeter through Strachan, 7/25/72, HRH Box 398.

89. Haldeman Diary, entry for 10/10/72.

90. Memo to Mitchell from Teeter, "Interim Analysis Report," 4/17/72, HRH Box 362.

91. Ibid.

92. Memo to Mitchell from Teeter, "Final First Wave Analysis," 5/11/72, HRH Box 362.

93. Memo to Mitchell from Teeter, "Interim Analysis Report," 4/17/72, HRH Box 362.

94. "Position Paper: The 1972 Campaign, 4/18/72," HRH Box 358.

95. Memo to Mitchell from Teeter, "Final First Wave Analysis," 5/11/72, HRH Box 362.

96. Memo to Mitchell from Teeter, "Campaign Theme," 4/12/72.

97. "Position Paper: The 1972 Campaign, 4/18/72," HRH Box 358.

98. Memo to Nixon from Colson, 1/19/72, PPF Box 16, marked "President seen" with handwritten note by Nixon "H[aldeman]—an excellent analysis.."

99. "Position Paper: The 1972 Campaign," 4/18/72, HRH Box 358.

100. Memo to Mitchell from Teeter, 4/12/72.

101. Memo to Haldeman from Teeter, 8/8/72, HRH Box 363.

102. Memo to Haldeman from Teeter, 8/8/72, HRH Box 363.

103. Popkin, *Reasoning Voter*; Rahn, "Candidate Evaluation in Complex Information Environments"; Miller, Wattenberg, and Malanchuk, "Schematic Assessments of Presidential Candidates"; Sniderman, Glaser, and Griffin, "Information and Electoral Choice."

104. Schumpeter, *Capitalism, Socialism, and Democracy*; Sartori, *Theory of Democracy Revisited.*

105. Page, *Choices and Echoes*; MacKuen, Erikson, and Stimson, "Peasants or Bankers?"

106. Jacobs, "The Presidency and the Press."

107. Jacobs and Shapiro, *Politicians Don't Pander.*

4

Continuing to Campaign: Public Opinion and the White House

Diane J. Heith

According to George Edwards, "the Clinton presidency is the ultimate example of . . . a presidency based on a perpetual campaign to obtain the public's support and fed by public opinion polls, focus groups, and public relations memos."[1] However, using polls to appeal to the public dates back to the Nixon administration. In 1980, Sidney Blumenthal argued that bringing polls and marketing to the White House represented a continuation of strategies learned on the campaign trail; hence his term for this behavior: "the permanent campaign."[2] Campaigning is inherently about persuasion—persuading an individual, or group of individuals, to vote. Therefore, Hugh Heclo argues that the permanent campaign (sometimes termed campaigning to govern) theory of presidential behavior merges the "power-as-persuasion inside Washington [theory] with power-as-public opinion manipulation outside Washington."[3] The resulting merger produces a different form of leadership because campaigning is inherently different from governing.

With a "polling apparatus," the White House gathers the public's attitudes for its own purposes.[4] Like modern campaigns, the use of opinion polls opens "the door of opportunity to orchestrate, amplify and inject the presumptive voices of the American people . . . into the daily management of public affairs."[5] Without polls, the candidate-centered campaigns of the late twentieth century and early twenty-first would not exist. Similarly, without a polling operation, presidential campaigning to govern could not exist.

Since Nixon, all presidents have internalized the lessons learned on the campaign trail. Successful presidential candidates bring their knowledge and dependence on the polls from the campaign trenches to the White House. Does the incorporation of polling produce permanent campaign leadership? The triumph of campaigning over governing within the presidency must begin with a switch from group-centered coalition building to self-centered strategizing. Traditionally, the president governs by assembling his party and interest groups on behalf of issues, policies, and legislation. In contrast, self-centered strategizing is presidency-centered, placing the president as the binding entity rather than an issue or bill before Congress. Similarly, modern campaigns are candidate-centered rather than party-centered. Moreover, self-centered strategizing during campaigns is completely dependent on poll-produced relationships. Therefore, evidence of the presidential permanent campaign begins with the retention of campaign techniques to maintain, expand, and utilize presidency-defined supporters. Using the presidential public opinion apparatus to define who is for and who is against the president is the most obvious, outward indicator of the permanent campaign. Instead of defining likely voters, presidents seek to define a base of support for the presidency as well as the presidential agenda.

The Nixon, Ford, Carter, Reagan, Bush I, and Clinton White Houses all employed the poll apparatus to define and monitor a presidency-centered coalition. The Nixon and Ford administrations used the polls to further define traditional descriptors of support. The Carter White House continued this evolution of the presidential coalition and defined members of the coalition by support for certain issues. The Reagan and Bush I administrations redefined the presidential constituency, reincorporating party ideologies and other identifiers. By the Clinton administration, the president, his consultants, and his staff were quite sophisticated in defining advocates and adversaries. Triangulation, the Clinton administration's constituency-based strategy, represents the epitome of an adversarial approach, which his successor, President George W. Bush, publicly repudiated and privately adopted.

Polling in the White House

The spending by the winning presidential candidate increased exponentially, from $25 million in 1968 to over $300 million in 2001.[6] The amount spent by presidential campaigns on public opinion polling also increased over time from $1.6 million by Richard Nixon in 1972 to almost $4 million in 1992. Similarly, Jacobs and Shapiro estimate that President Nixon, while in the White House, spent over $5 million (in 1995 inflation adjusted dollars) on public opinion polling data.[7]

Patrick Caddell received over $1.3 million between 1977 and 1979 for polling for President Carter.[8] In 1981 alone, Richard Wirthlin received $820,000 polling for Ronald Reagan.[9] The Bush polling budget was $650,000 in 1989 for quarterly national surveys by Robert Teeter.[10] President Clinton spent over $15 million on public polls during his two terms in the White House.[11] With this significant outlay of party funds, these White Houses created a polling operation.

Public attitudes have always been important to presidents. The White House has always received information about the public from a variety of sources: the media, the party, other elites, and, of course, the presidential mailbag. Straw polls and canvassing have been commonplace with American officials since the 1700s.[12] Presidents as early as Hoover and FDR sought quantitative representations of the public's attitudes. Hoover had his White House staff do a content analysis, relatively sophisticated for its time, of the editorial pages of newspapers.[13] Without the benefit of polls or statistics, Hoover effectively sampled opinion of the day.[14] It was only in the 1930s that the modern presidential polling apparatus first emerged,[15] yet, the White House did not institutionalize polling until after the high-level intelligence gathering involved in John F. Kennedy's 1960 run for the presidency.[16] The Kennedy and Johnson administrations dramatically increased interest in public and private administration polling, primarily for elections, but also for governing.[17] Jacobs and Shapiro argue that the Kennedy and Johnson administrations, marked by their infrequent poll usage, were quantifiably different from the institutionalized efforts evident in the post-Johnson presidencies.[18] In stark contrast, the administrations of Nixon, Ford, Carter, Reagan, Bush I and Clinton devoted substantial time, money, and attention to a White House public opinion apparatus. The polls aided White House efforts to extend their electoral coalitions. However, how those administrations employed the polls to define and use their electoral coalition changed dramatically over time.

Nixon and Ford: Partisanship Loses Its Centrality

Despite trying to deny members of his party access to poll data,[19] the Nixon administration began its public tracking utilizing traditional survey variables: party identification, religion, race, and geography. In addition to these typical socioeconomic status (SES) variables, the White House evaluated current and future support for Nixon, his policies, and his reelection. Age and location on the liberal-conservative spectrum rounded out the coalition analysis in the early 1970s.[20]

Over the course of the Nixon administration, the classification and tracking of the American public gradually became more detailed and less committed to party descriptors. The first significant addition to the variable list was the phrase, the "Silent Majority."[21] The Silent Majority captured attitudes contrary to those of the students protesting against the Vietnam War. The White House also expanded its traditional demographic markers to include new measures of economic status. Nixon once noted to John Ehrlichman that "people who live in homes that they own tend to take a much more conservative view on public issues than people who rent. I think this has significant consequences as far as our own programs are concerned. . . . I would like you to follow through in any way that you think would be appropriate to reach our homeowner constituency."[22] Thus, Nixon's staff hunted for advocates among poll-produced constituencies by considering things like lifestyle in addition to the traditional SES variables.

The premise behind the development of the permanent campaign is that the methodology and values of campaigning are so pervasive and compelling that they come to dominate governing. President Ford entered office with no presidential campaign experience and thus no permanent campaign to import. Consequently, across all traditional SES categories, the pollster Robert Teeter continued to find that "the President has not created any Ford constituency unique from that of any Republican President."[23] The age category, however, offered hope, as "the one exception to this is that he does show unique strength with young voters for a Republican."[24]

In search of a "unique constituency," the Ford pollsters began employing the more segmented view of society favored by the end of Nixon's tenure. They abandoned the simple tracking of party identification as they became aware of the declining efficacy of the party identification variable for voters, something they learned from candidate experiences as well as from political scientists. Robert Goldwin, of the office of President Ford's chief of staff, had a conversation with Professor Norman Nie in September 1975. In a four-page summary of that conversation, Goldwin informed Donald Rumsfeld and Richard Cheney of the political scientist's views on the declining potency of parties and the increased potency of issues.[25] Moreover, Goldman, in summarizing Nie's statements, noted, "[T]here seem to be tendencies toward greater ethnic awareness, [and] the general ties of ethnic groups to party identification and to issues seem to be breaking down."[26] The Nixon, Carter, Reagan, and Bush I administrations were similarly attentive to the observations of political science scholars identifying a breakdown in traditional categorizations.

Accordingly, the Ford White House tracked those they defined as "major sub groups": northern and southern WASPs, Roman Catholics, Jews, and blacks. The WASPs and Roman Catholics were further divided by age and education.[27] Like the Nixon administration, the nontraditional categories appear to be directly related to certain issue areas. For example, on energy issues "Total Americans who work outside the home" was a separate category. For questions concerning college education, individuals were asked if they had children. However, the Ford approach appeared more haphazard than Nixon's; it became more like a "search and rescue" mission than an effort to define constituent support.

Carter: The Horse You Rode In On

Under Patrick Caddell's tutelage, the Carter administration immediately refashioned Nixon and Ford's modified SES and party tracking. In the 1976 election, Carter won traditional Democratic support from Catholics, Jews, blacks, labor, the poor, and drew votes from traditionally Democratic geographic areas like Chicago, but "he may owe his election more to the non-traditional groups (white Protestants, the better educated, white collar, and rural, small-town voters) that helped him to do better in unexpected places."[28] Voters age 25–35, nonworking housewives, and those from the West deserted Carter in droves during the 1976 campaign.[29]

The Carter administration disaggregated his supporters far beyond SES categories to include lifestyle choices and extended the linkages of those new categories to Carter's issues, like energy. "Caddell cross-tabulated answers to questions on Carter's energy policy with traditional respondent characteristics and also the type of home heating utilized by the respondent. The White House believed that the type of home heating mattered for support for various energy programs and options for conservation."[30] However, the White House never discovered support for the president or his energy policies amongst the public as a whole or in any segment of home-heating users.

Reagan and Bush I: The Bull's-eye Approach

The process of identifying and tracking a presidentially defined constituency continued to evolve. Nixon began and Carter continued a process designed to assess the depth of support across numerous unnatural demographics alongside presidential policies. The Reagan and Bush administrations continued this approach but added their own twist, or refinement, to the Nixon approach. The Reagan and Bush administrations used polling to define, to identify, and to track supporters in terms of the relationship to strength of support for the president, which they separated into core and peripheral support. Peripheral support required the constant monitoring that only public opinion polling can provide, since support from weak-identifiers is transitory. "Peripheral supporters can be appealed to only on the issues of concern to them, and their demands may constrain a president's option and even conflict with the preferences of the president's core coalition."[31]

The Reagan White House used the polling apparatus to segment individuals even farther than Nixon or Carter, adding ethnicity and religious categories (including born-again status).[32] The Reagan White House classified the president's supporters in order to monitor that support over time. "Strategic Planning Memorandum #3" outlined in some detail the importance of a constituency strategy. It contained twenty-four recommendations for the president's 1982 State of the Union address. Richard Beal argued that "Eleanor and Joe Q. Public . . . are the ultimate members of the coalitions the President will need to accomplish his goals and visions."[33] Polling was central to encapsulating these individuals, because "these coalitions must be thought of in terms of geography as well as individual and group identity."[34] Only polling reveals the level of detail necessary to track these classifications. Unlike traditional public identifying assertions, like voting or party affiliation, polling allows presidents and their staffs to monitor private, unspoken affiliations like age, income, religion, and homeownership.

Using the Reagan baseline aided efforts to pass the 1982 budget. Reagan staffers closely monitored reactions to the president's proposals, but not simply for public relations purposes. "Support for continuing to cut domestic spending as a means to balance the budget and improve the economy centers in the core of Reagan support group: Republicans, westerners, southerners, upper income earners, high church Protestants, and men. The problem is, these alone do not constitute an electoral majority. The group that took Reagan over the top in 1980 is the group that has begun to shift toward defense cuts. These include the old voters (45–64 years of age), those with some college experience, middle to upper income earners, Midwesterners, some high church Protestants, those who are ideologically somewhat conservative or moderate, and weak Democrats."[35] Richard Beal highlighted the importance of defining adversaries and advocates in order to satisfy the presidential reelection imperative. The president and his staff linked reelection directly to retaining the initial Reagan baseline.

Table 4.1
Reagan Coalitions' Network Preferences

Network	Supporters
CBS	Best Educated
	Blacks
	Registered independents
	Residents of Southern States
NBC	Senior citizens
	Lower-Income individuals
	Registered Republicans
ABC	Youngest viewers
	High school graduates
	Blue collar
	Blacks
	Democrats

Source: Memo to Meese, Baker, Deaver from Wirthlin, 2/2/82, in PR 15 doc. #061990, Ronald Reagan Library.

Thus, Reagan's policy strategy and reelection strategy relied heavily on presidential appeals to the public. Recognizing that the media served as an intermediary between the president and the public, the Reagan White House even wanted to know which columnists, newscasters, anchors, and networks their supporters preferred. As of 2 February 1982, the public preferred CBS by a narrow margin (26 % over ABC with 25% and 23% for NBC). Interestingly, "Jack Anderson and William Buckley have close to the same visibility and the same thermometer ratings despite significant differences on the ideological backgrounds of the two columnists."[36] The administration broke down support for the networks and columnists by the Reagan coalition categories. Mixed- and low-support groups primarily watched NBC and ABC (see table 4.1). Responsiveness and attention to constituent attitudes were pervasive, even coloring the vehicle through which the White House spread its message. Moreover, as indicated by the dissection of media approval, any type of targeting was possible once the administration established the baseline. Without the understanding of an electoral coalition, in this case Reagan's, any information that categorizes by groups becomes less significant.

The George H. W. Bush campaign and White House borrowed significantly from the Reagan method of classifying supporters, despite doing less constituency tracking. The Bush staff further subdivided the conception of the core and periphery model of constituents. The Bush administration divided the core (which they called the base) into four groups: political, ethnic and demographic, geographic, and issue-oriented

Table 4.2
The Bush Constituency

Political	Geographic	Issue-oriented
Republicans	California, Texas, Southern states	Law enforcement
Conservatives	Rocky Mountain states	Veterans, national defense groups
Republican officeholders	New England (sans RI)	Teamsters, conservative union members
Bush supporters		Social value groups
		Small business, entrpreneurs
Ethnic/Demographic		Corporate trade associations
Asians		Conservationists
European 1st–4th generation		Evangelicals
Northern Catholics		Antitax organizations
Younger voters		

Source: Memo to Sununu from Demarest in Sununu Box 3, Persian Gulf Working Groups OA/ID CF 00472, George Bush Library.

(table 4.2 contains the base breakdown). The Bush staff contrasted the base with target groups in the same categories. Conservative Democrats represented political target groups, while blacks, Hispanics, and seniors fell into the all-encompassing ethnic/demographic category.[37] Pollster Robert Teeter termed Bush's constituency "the expected Republican coalition: putting together large majorities of Northern white Protestants and Southern whites with a smaller majority of Catholics and over 40% of union families. Blacks, Jews, and Hispanics again went overwhelmingly Democratic."[38] These traditional social divisions dominated, as Teeter argued the "baby boomers" and "Reagan Democrats" were not useful constructs in 1988.[39]

The similarity to the Reagan constituency classification efforts ends here. The Bush classification system was more general. For example, the Bush administration polled for religion but dropped Reagan's classification system in favor of the generic (Active Protestants, Inactive Protestant, Active Catholic, Inactive Catholic, Jewish, and Non-religious).[40] Although the Bush staff tracked ticket-splitters, conservative Republicans, and conservative Democrats,[41] unlike Carter and Reagan, the Bush administration rarely employed innovative or distinctive sub-group terminology.

Clinton: Evolving Back to the Campaign

President Clinton's electoral coalition was a mix of the traditional and nontraditional. His core support came from traditional Democratic sources: party identifiers, liberals, nonwhites, women, Easterners, and those with lower incomes (there were no linkages to age or education).[42] Clinton, according to Edwards, " polarized the public along partisan lines."[43] Moreover, in 1992, Democrats turned out and Republicans stayed home.[44] In addition, the Democrat's appeal to independents and moderates, as well as the siphoning created by the Perot vote, produced the Clinton victory. The demographics Clinton could not include in his conglomeration of support were the wealthy, white Protestants, born-again Christians, and homemakers.[45] "Thus . . . [Clinton] took office with a very weak governing coalition and a campaign commitment to a dramatic first hundred days."[46]

The Clinton administration polled continually throughout its first term, tracking a variety of demographic groups. The Morris memoranda in *Behind the Oval Office* demonstrate an intensive, detailed tracking of supporters, nonsupporters, and those on the fence. For example, the Clinton pollsters used polls and focus groups to identify "swing Democrats" and Independent voters in Louisiana, Minneapolis, New York, and Florida.[47] The Clinton administration was extremely attentive to the "20% of vote that is up for grabs."[48] The White House used the poll data to "focus on expanding [its] base, not just strengthening it."[49]

Over time, the Clinton team tried to compensate for the heterogeneity of the presidential coalition by connecting constituents' attitudes with presidential rhetorical efforts—in other words, they adopted a campaign style of leadership. Two cases illustrate the growth by the Clinton White House toward a new breed of leadership. The 1993–94 Clinton health care effort demonstrates traditional, rather than campaign, leadership. The Clinton health care effort remained within a group-centered governing focus. The 1995 budget battle with congressional Republicans reveals the evolution toward self-centered strategizing and campaigning to govern.

HEALTH CARE. When Bill Clinton took office as president, health care was already on the agenda. Beliefs concerning containing costs, guaranteeing fair access, and the "appropriateness of political intervention" converged to produce a favorable climate for presidential action.[50] Scholars have also argued that while the timing was right for the issue of health care, by 1994 the environment for presidential action was weak.[51] President Clinton seized his opportunity; but as is axiomatic in politics, it did not work out the way the White House planned. Instead, the Clinton health care package, the centerpiece of his agenda, unraveled for reasons as diverse as concerns over government involvement, quality of care, physician choice, medical costs, and interest-group mobilization.[52]

The fundamental difference between a campaign approach and a governing approach to presidential leadership centers around the relationship between the president and his constituents. Candidates use public opinion surveys to determine what encourages or discourages behavior. Candidates lead by stating who they are and what their stands are on the issues. Candidates follow by tinkering with their message or their appearance. Generally, it is this ongoing redefinition and repositioning of the candidate that hallmarks any campaign. Although the health care effort was presidency-centered, the Clinton White House did not tinker with his constituency, only with his language.

The Clinton White House began the health care process from a governing perspective, despite the presence of so many campaign workers and a president predisposed to utilizing polls. The White House delegated a task force, led by Hillary Clinton, and Ira Magaziner, to define the president's first big legislative campaign. The public was virtually excluded from the policymaking process. Jacobs and Shapiro contend that public opinion was a tool "to craft the presentation of Clinton's plan—a plan that had been formulated to reflect the President's philosophy, policy preferences, and political judgments."[53] However, Clinton's pollster, Stan Greenberg, was out of the loop during policy formulation. "Greenberg complained that the preferences of most Americans had been sacrificed to Clinton's policy goals."[54] The Clinton White House used polls and focus groups to try to frame their arguments and style the language and symbols used in presidential rhetoric.[55] "The bottom line is that polls and focus groups did not—according to a senior health policy adviser—'enter into the decision' about adopting an employer mandate and rejecting a payroll tax. . . . Indeed, one senior health policy official suggested that the uncertainty about the future strengthened the White House's focus on 'policy integrity' and its inclination to discount existing or anticipated public opinion."[56]

Unlike the self-centered strategizing employed during his presidential campaign, Clinton played heed to traditional Democratic constituents and significant interest groups in the health care debate. Long-term care and a prescription drug plan appealed to seniors and the American Association for Retired Persons (AARP) as well as to "small businesses, urban areas, provider groups, and single-payer advocates."[57] In terms of the mass public, the Clinton White House sought the generic, ill-defined middle class.

Thus, the Clinton White House did not define the content of the health care proposals utilizing a campaign-style leadership approach, determined by presidency-centered strategizing. Rather, the Clinton

White House employed what Jacobs and Shapiro define as "crafted talk," which appears to be a form of the perpetual campaign, yet is not due to the timing and ramifications of the polling usage. As Jacobs and Shapiro articulate, the motivation for employing public opinion polls is "neither to follow [public opinion] in making decisions nor to accept it as it existed."[58] A crafted talk approach seeks to shape public opinion and sell a proposal, after defining the policy. The perpetual-campaign style of leadership begins with the constituency and moves toward an agenda. Crafted talk and the rhetorical presidency begin with the agenda and move toward groups and individuals.

The White House did use polls to make the complex health care debate personal, but generically personal—partially in order "to preempt the media's portrayal of the personal consequences of Clinton's plan and to neutralize journalists' expected focus on how the plan would affect everyday Americans."[59] But more often than not, polling helped the White House identify the favorable and the unfavorable and pitch their proposals accordingly. For example, the polls demonstrated that the public supported "universal coverage" but did not support "promises to control costs and government bureaucracy."[60] The White House related public support to individual interest, but from this universal perspective. "Pitching reform to the public's self-interest was a persistent theme in the reports prepared by Stan Greenberg. President Clinton's own statements emphasized the implications for individuals—how they would gain financially and retain the same quality of care."[61] Thus, the building of a multilayered health care program remained centered in traditional presidential persuasive efforts. The health care fight may have looked like a campaign as the White House polled continually and designed a strategy to sell a program that appealed to citizen concerns. Upon careful inspection, however, the battle for health care lacked the crucial component for campaigning to govern: self-centered constituent strategizing.

THE BUDGET SHOWDOWN. The high point of polling and campaigning within the Clinton administration clearly came during the Dick Morris era and efforts to "triangulate" the public. Triangulation has received a lot of coverage, due in part to its emphasis on capturing the middle rather than the traditional method of building out from the party core. According to Dick Morris, "triangulation demanded that Clinton abandon 'Democratic class-warfare dogma,' rise above his partisan roots, and inhabit the political center 'above and between' the two parties. . . . That meant Clinton had to deliberately distance himself from his Democratic allies, use them as a foil, pick fights with them."[62] As a presidential strategy, triangulation caused dissension in the White House ranks and produced murky results—for instance, the public's issue positions suggested action but Clinton received no corresponding upward movement of his popularity ratings.[63]

Triangulation represents the ultimate extension of a campaign approach, because it embodies the defining of supporters with an acknowledgment of single-point-in-time goals. According to Morris, Clinton's use of polls did not identify "what should I be for? What should I do?" Clinton knew what he wanted to do; he wanted to know how to get there. The poll data lit the path—just as in a presidential campaign. Instead of focusing on traditional Democrats and their goals, the Clinton White House targeted the goals that overlapped with other constituencies. From the polls, Morris and Clinton determined that "massive majorities consistently rejected the doctrinaire views of both the left and the right and embraced an amalgam of conservative and liberal positions."[64] Clinton began his odyssey by flirting with the New Democrats rather than joining the more moderate wing of the Democratic Party.[65] "The President in effect pursued a 'median voter' strategy of adopting positions on salient issues that were closest to the midpoint of public opinion in order to show most voters that they would benefit from his reelection."[66]

Triangulation demanded an expansive polling effort, which was entirely presidency-centered. Support from the center is not instinctively identifiable, as are core party supporters. Traditional governing coalitions stem from their relationship to ideas and interests, like the Christian Right and the Republicans or Labor and the Democrats. The middle represents those individuals who fall between other clear identifiers – the middle-of-the-road opinion is not apparent without those traditional end points. Clinton and Morris built a triangulated constituency centered on trumping the president's opponents. Traditional issues, policy, and even the 1996 election were secondary steps.

The battle between the Clinton White House and the congressional Republicans, led by Speaker Newt Gingrich, to balance the budget culminated in 1995 with a government shutdown. This fight encapsulated a campaign approach to presidential leadership. Balancing the budget was not a Democratic ideal. The Clinton White House began with an artificial linkage between issues and constituencies, determined by the polls; added a hostile Republican Party; and campaigned for victory.

Campaign-style leadership began with Dick Morris who used the balancing of the budget issue as a mechanism to produce a presidency-centered coalition designed as a stepping-stone to the 1996 election—to the dismay of the rest of the White House.[67] The core of the Clinton

White House, especially the staffers who were a part of the Clinton campaign, were ideologically opposed to balancing the budget. Since FDR and the creation of social government spending, national budgets, for the most part, have not balanced, regardless of which party has controlled the government. The idea of balancing the budget and a balanced budget amendment gathered steam as part of the conservatism of the Reagan Republicans. Ironically, the Reagan and Bush era tripled the national debt through the combination of supply-side economics and increased military spending.

Morris argued that triangulation was the key to a Clinton victory in the 1996 election and that the balanced-budget was a crucial component in that strategy. The budget was critical to defeating the Republicans, according to Morris, because the ideas behind their balanced-budget fervor betrayed the public. "The president suspected, and I agreed, that the Republicans were not cutting Medicare, Medicaid, education, and environmental protection—areas the president cared about—in order to balance the budget. They wanted to balance the budget *in order* to cut Medicare, Medicaid, education, and environmental protection. . . . On the other hand, the Democrats were protecting these programs as an excuse *not* to balance the budget."[68] Thus, the budget was a way to beat everyone politically and at the polls—triangulation at its best.

At its heart, triangulation lacks any ideology or goal beyond victory. For Morris and Clinton, the balanced budget would be the key to Clinton's victory in 1996 because it created a link between constituencies, issues, and Clinton himself. Morris defended his approach to others inside and outside the administration. "My role in this process was to see where the budget numbers were leading him and, through polling, vet it politically. . . . I also found that voters didn't really care whether the budget was balanced in seven, eight, nine or even ten years. It didn't matter to them as long as we moved in the right direction."[69] Clinton wanted to balance the budget because the public wanted it. Moreover, how the budget would be balanced was determined with reelection in mind. Unlike the crafted talk approach to health care, the Clinton White House went to the polls much earlier in the balanced budget legislative battle. Unlike health care, the primary goal here was to beat the Republicans and not necessarily to pass policy.

The Clinton team used polls to design speeches, and public opinion even influenced the critical decision to shut down the government via presidential vetoes. In May 1995, Dick Morris pressed for a speech on the budget, because "the key to getting that ten percent—the swing vote, the Perot vote—is to give a prime-time speech. It has to be next week, or we lose them forever."[70] "And they gave the speech on balancing the budget the following Tuesday which 'triangulated with a vengeance.'"[71] After the president's speeches on the balanced budget, the rest of the fight was played out behind the scenes—the president and Senate Majority Leader Bob Dole wanted a deal. However, the 1994 freshman Republicans in the House of Representatives did not.[72]

During the 14–19 November 1995 government shutdown, the White House polling operation went into overdrive. In *Behind the Oval Office*, Morris writes that he polled every night during the crisis. Morris, George Stephanopoulos, and President Clinton all started their day with "the latest polling information."[73] The polling numbers showed record approval ratings for the Clinton administration. More importantly, the public did not approve of the Republican tactics. Morris does note, however, that he urged a deal on the budget after the numbers began to show "impatience with the continued stalemate."[74]

President Clinton's balanced-budget program was steeped in poll data and campaign-style leadership. The bulk of the White House staff opposed balancing the budget, in accord with traditional Democratic principles. Armed with poll data supporting balancing the budget, Morris pushed for the program. President Clinton clearly had to balance not only the budget but also the competing advice he was receiving from his trusted sources. Interestingly, the balanced budget effort was both a "repudiation and a vindication" of triangulation, as the poll numbers rewarded the line-in-the-sand approach (e.g., the vetoes that shut the government down) and penalized accommodation (e.g., the handshake deal with Newt Gingrich in New Hampshire).[75] Thus, the effort was classic permanent campaign strategy.

Bush II: The Appearance of Repudiation

In his acceptance speech at the Republican National Convention, George W. Bush passionately distanced himself from Clinton's polling presidency: "I believe great decisions are made with care, made with conviction, not made with polls," said Bush; "I do not need to take your pulse before I know my own mind." Publicly, Bush rejected the "permanent campaign" stylings of the Clinton era. However, Kathryn Tenpas and Stephen Hess of the Brookings Institution argue that once in office the forty-third president "out-Clintoned Clinton" by instituting an Office of Strategic Initiatives (OSI). OSI exists to expand Bush's electoral coalition and monitor the Republican base.[76]

Like Gerald Ford, Bush entered office with a problematic electoral coalition. The Electoral College victory without a popular vote victory plagued the Bush White House. The 2000 battle between Vice President Al Gore and then governor George W. Bush was fascinating to observers for its lack of change in the trial-heat polls. From September 2000 to Election Day 2000, the polls revealed remarkably similar results. Approximately 45% of eligible voters were prepared to vote for Bush, and approximately 45% of eligible voters planned to vote for Gore. The remaining 10 to 15% were unsure. The split between the candidates reflected the distribution of Republicans, Democrats, and independents across the country. As Wilson McWilliams argues, "both parties attempted to reach beyond their traditional bases, and both pretty much failed."[77]

Thus, Bush entered office with an electoral coalition reflecting the complexities of the 2000 campaign. Bush earned office primarily via the votes of white men and married white women. He made some gains with Catholics and Hispanics.[78] "African Americans, Jews, about two-thirds of Hispanics, and a majority of Asians . . . union members and unmarried women" voted for Gore.[79] A geographic split matched the dramatic demographic split. Bush won the South and the Prairie and Mountain West, while Gore won the big cites and the coasts. The geographic disparity produced a striking United States electoral map with blue-edges and a red-middle. Consequently, Bush entered office with a poorly constructed electoral coalition that posed myriad problems for governing.

Lacking a mandate and a large base of support, the Bush White House was forced to be attentive to a polling apparatus for coalition building purposes while continuing publicly to reject the need to do so. The first nine months of the president's tenure mirrored the divisions established in the campaign. The president's public statements began reflecting the difficulty in leading without a large percentage of committed supporters. On 20 March 2001, Bush claimed, "We set out a set of principles and stand by them. . . . We don't use polls and focus groups to figure out where to head."[80] By the end of April, Bush noted, "[Y]ou read these polls. They're saying, you know, 'Do you want to take away somebody's Social Security check, or do you want to have tax relief?' But that's not the choice."[81] Bush's early statements and decisive shifts in policy positions, particularly on the environment and energy, cost him in the polls and forced him to change his strategy. The Bush White House initially tossed out positions such as scaling back limitations on arsenic and scrapping a promise to curb carbon dioxide emissions, and then quickly reversed them or shifted its ground to appear environmental. The White House proposed, the public reacted, and the administration adjusted. Clearly, the White House was attentive to both supporters and critics.

The Bush team spent much of its first nine months dancing around the efforts to employ public opinion while still trying to distance themselves from the Clinton poll-driven presidency. Andrew Card, Bush's chief of staff, informed reporters that the Bush White House was not concerned with polls, but rather with *marketing*. Therefore, "if a policy goes amok, it may not be the policy that is at fault, Card suggested, but flawed marketing."[82] Repeatedly, the White House insisted that Bush would not use the polls as Clinton did. "He still won't govern by polls, says White House press secretary Ari Fleischer. He's aware of them, but he doesn't lead by the polls. He leads by what he thinks is right for America."[83] However, Stephen Hess contends that Bush "does seem to be tacking back to where the polls are. . . . It's as if we've watched the first George W. Bush presidency yield to the second."[84]

In his first months in office, Bush "failed to ease the partisan divisions in the country . . . frustrating administration efforts to enlarge his fragile political base and prompting advisers to look for ways to redefine his presidency."[85] To expand the coalition, Bush desperately needed independents. Like Clinton, Bush was sharply polarizing; he was immensely popular with his own party and despised by Democrats. Karl Rove and OSI planned a Fall 2001 offensive "aimed at carving out a different kind of orthodoxy for the party."[86] Rove's plans sounded very similar to Patrick Caddell's and Dick Morris's efforts to assemble presidency-centered coalitions for Jimmy Carter and Bill Clinton, respectively.[87] If not for the terrorist attacks on 11 September 2001, the Bush White House likely would have undertaken a permanent-campaign approach to governing.

In the wake of September 11th, the problem of working with the public paradoxically eased for the Bush administration. The president now had a war to fight and a nation to calm. However, after the worst attack on the United States since Pearl Harbor, public support for its president surged. In classic "rally-around-the-flag" response, the public offered President Bush stratospheric approval ratings. Terrorism easily muted much of the debate about the public and its mixed support for the president. By the midterm of his administration, Bush's popularity fell approximately twenty percentage points to the 70% range. In July 2001, Matthew Dowd, the Republican National Committee's director of polling, claimed that a "sharply polarized electorate . . . means that the president will rarely have approval ratings about 60% and that about one-third of the country will say they disapprove of how he is doing his job."[88] Thus, terrorism accomplished what the White House marketing team could not: bringing together the country behind the President and his proscribed course of action.

Conclusions

Polling stands at the heart of the modern, candidate-centered presidential campaign, thus making it a fitting proxy for evaluating the presence of a permanent campaign environment within the White House. In an era of declining party identification and loyalty, public opinion polls and the polling consultant represent critical components of a successful campaign. Careful identification of supporters and nonsupporters depends on the ability to discern who backs the candidate and why. Presidents Nixon, Ford, Carter, Reagan, G. H. W. Bush, Clinton, and G. W. Bush clearly transferred their campaign polling apparatus to the White House. This chapter demonstrates that the White House also imported the first step of any campaign: defining support.

These seven White Houses classified and categorized individuals via public opinion polling. The component at the heart of the presidential classification effort was not voter mobilization but rather support for the president and his policies. Using the poll apparatus, these administrations attempted to define their unique presidential constituency. The hunt for the presidential coalition began with the traditional demographic dissections: party identification and socioeconomic variables. Over time, the White House increasingly segmented the presidential constituency by issues and ultimately by nontraditional socioeconomic factors. Thus, via the polling apparatus, these White Houses meet the first criteria for a permanent-campaign leadership strategy. The polling apparatus, which could disaggregate individuals limited only by the questions asked, permitted a continuation of the leadership strategy that presidents learned on the campaign trail: connect individuals to the president based not on party affiliation, but on disconnected affiliations ranging from individual attributes, to lifestyle choices, to presidential policy positions.

Creating coalitions that place the president as the fulcrum are nothing new. Poll-defined constituencies, however, do not exist in the political sphere outside of the pollster's reports, charts, tables, and memoranda. Home-owning individuals, home-heating constituencies, or soccer moms never mobilize on their own—there are no marches on Washington to vocalize demands. The highly fractured approach to the president's constituencies challenges traditional perceptions of the presidency and the presidential audience.[89] In the traditional typology—which distinguishes the common, constituent, and partisan approaches—the common audience refers to the president's unique relationship with the entire country. Constituent patrons are "specific groups within the broader national community," such as the American Association for Retired Persons, while partisan audiences by definition stem from the president's party.[90] The triangulation approach, employed by the Clinton White House, ignores these traditional relationships and fashions new ones. Thus, the "coalition" produced by the polling is manufactured for a single point in time, in Clinton's case to triumph over the Republicans on the issue of the balanced budget.

Leadership, based upon alliances that do not exist outside of a survey, is fragile and ultimately a problem for democracy. A fragmented ideology, such as triangulation, challenges governing, as presidents do not truly mobilize or motivate citizens in support of anything beyond themselves. This is demagoguery, not democracy. Triangulation is the ideological equivalent of a Chinese menu: select one from Column A and two from Column B. This style of leadership can be compelling and can work. However, it is a short-term solution lacking any grounding in ideology, especially traditional party ideology.

Notes

1. Edwards, "Campaigning Is Not Governing," p. 33.

2. Blumenthal, *Permanent Campaign*.

3. Heclo, "Campaigning and Governing," p. 29.

4. Jacobs, "The Recoil Effect."

5. Heclo, "Campaigning and Governing," pp. 25-26.

6. The Center for Responsive Politics, "All Presidential Candidates."

7. Jacobs and Shapiro, "The Rise of Presidential Polling," p. 171.

8. Bonafede, "A Pollster to the President"; Federal Election Commission, Party Disclosure documents, 1980–2000.

9. Bonafede, "A Pollster to the President"; Federal Election Commission, Party Disclosure documents, 1980–2000.

10. Memo to Wray from Matalin, 8/4/89, in PR 13-8 062870-06609ss, George Bush Library.

11. Federal Election Commission, Party Disclosure documents, 1980–2000.

12. Jacobs, "The Recoil Effect."

13. Eisinger, "Gauging Public Opinion in the Hoover White House."

14. Ibid.

15. Jacobs, "The Recoil Effect."

16. Ibid.

17. Jacobs and Shapiro, "The Rise of Presidential Polling."

18. Jacobs and Shapiro, "Issue, Candidate Image, and Priming"; Jacobs and Shapiro, "The Rise of Presidential Polling"; Jacobs and Shapiro, "Public Decisions, Private Polls."

19. Heith, "Staffing the White House Public Opinion Apparatus."

20. Heith, "Presidential Polling and the Potential for Leadership," p. 384.

21. Ibid., p. 387

22. Memo to Ehrlichman from Nixon, 3/10/73, in WHSF Box 18, Ehrlichman Nixon Presidential Papers.

23. Memo to Cheney from Teeter, 11/12/75, in Hartmann Papers Box 163, Public Opinion Polling General (1), Gerald R. Ford Library.

24. Memo to Cheney from Teeter, 11/12/75, in Hartmann Papers Box 163, Public Opinion Polling General (1), Gerald R. Ford Library.

25. Memo to Rumsfeld, Cheney from Goldwin, 9/30/75, in Robert Goldman Papers Box 26, Norman Nie, Gerald R. Ford Library.

26. Ibid.

27. "Responses to Cynicism Items" in Teeter Box 51, U.S. National 2/75 Foreword and Overview, Gerald R. Ford Library.

28. Memo to Carter from Caddell, 12/7/76, Cabinet Selection, Political Problems, in 11176–1/77 Box 1, Handwriting File, p.13, Jimmy Carter Library.

29. Heith, "Presidential Polling and the Potential for Leadership," p. 385.

30. Ibid., p. 387.

31. Seligman and Covington, *Coalitional Presidency*, p. 13.

32. Heith, "Presidential Polling and the Potential for Leadership."

33. Memo to Meese, Baker, Deaver from Beal, 10/2/81, in SP 230 doc. # 580230, Ronald Reagan Library.

34. Ibid.

35. Memo to Meese, Baker, Deaver, Clark from Beal, 3/12/82, Strategic Evaluation Memorandum #13 Ronald Reagan Library.

36. Memo to Meese, Baker, Deaver from Wirthlin, 2/2/82, in PR 15 doc. # 061990, Ronald Reagan Library.

37. Memo to Sununu from Demarest, 12/2/90, in Sununu Box 3, Persian Gulf Working Groups OA/ID CF 00472, George Bush Library.

38. 1988 Presidential Election Thematic Components, in Sununu Box 13, 1990 Polling OA/ID CF 00153 1 of 3, George Bush Library, p. 6.

39. Ibid.

40. Memo to Porter from Goldstein, 9/28/90, in Ed Goldstein Files, Public Opinion 1991 OA/ID 06681 2 of 2, George Bush Library.

41. Memo to Card, Demarest, Fitzwater, Kristol, Porter and Rogich from Rogers, 10/24/89, in Sig Rogich Files [Campaign Polls OA/ID o4732 1 of 2]; Memo to Darman from Scully, 4/26/91, in Sununu polling 2 of 3 199, George Bush Library.

42. Wayne, *Road to the White House, 1996*; Edwards, "Frustration and Folly."

43. Edwards, "Frustration and Folly," p. 236.

44. Wayne, *Road to the White House*. 1996.

45. Ibid.

46. Smith, "Redefining the Rhetorical Presidency," p. 228; Cohen, *Changing Course in Washington*.

47. Morris, *Behind the Oval Office*, p. 409. The Nixon, Ford, and Carter administrations did not utilize focus groups at all. The Reagan and Bush I White Houses appear to have employed focus groups in their campaigns, but I did not find more than occasional references to them within the White House memoranda.

48. Morris, *Behind the Oval Office*, p. 361.

49. Ibid., p. 363.

50. Disch, "Publicity-Stunt Participation and Sound Bite Polemics"; Skocpol, "The Aftermath of Defeat."

51. Heclo, "The Clinton Health Plan"; Morone, "The Administration of Health Care Reform"; Skocpol, "The Rise and Resounding Demise of the Clinton Plan."

52. West, Heith, and Goodwin, "Harry and Louise Go To Washington."

53. Jacobs and Shapiro, *Politicians Don't Pander*, p. 102.

54. Ibid., p. 97.

55. Ibid., p. 102.

56. Ibid., p. 100.

57. Ibid., p. 100.

58. Ibid., p. 103.

59. Ibid., p. 111.

60. Ibid., p. 110.

61. Ibid., p. 260.

62. Stephanopoulos, *All Too Human*, p. 334.

63. Edsall, "Confrontation Is the Key to Clinton's Popularity."

64. Morris, *Behind the Oval Office*, p. 208.

65. Stephanopoulos, *All Too Human*, p. 198.

66. Edsall, "Confrontation Is the Key to Clinton's Popularity."

67. Morris does note, however, that Erskine Bowles, Bill Curry, Don Baer, and Bruce Reed were supportive of a balanced budget (*Behind the Oval Office*).

68. Italics in original. Morris, *Behind the Oval Office*, p. 161.

69. Ibid., p. 165.

70. Stephanopoulos, *All Too Human*, p. 350.

71. Ibid., p. 358.

72. An excellent discussion of the Republican stand can be found in Killian, *Freshman*.

73. Morris, *Behind the Oval Office*, p. 183.

74. Ibid., p. 185.

75. Edsall, "Confrontation Is the Key to Clinton's Popularity."

76. Tenpas and Hess, "Bush's A Team."

77. McWilliams, "The Meaning of the Election," p. 184.

78. Ibid.

79. Ibid., pp. 184–85.

80. Simendinger, "In His Own (Mixed) Words," p. 1249.

81. Ibid.

82. McAllister, "Bush Polls Apart from Clinton in Use of Marketing," p. A-14.

83. Fritz, "As Bush Sinks in Polls," p. A1.

84. Ibid.

85. Balz, "Partisan Divisions Bedevil Bush," p. A1.

86. Ibid.

87. See Heith, *Polling for Policy* for a discussion of Caddell's plans.

88. Balz, "Partisan Divisions Bedevil Bush," p. A01.

89. King and Ragsdale, *Elusive Executive*.

90. Ibid.

5

Do Polls Give the Public a Voice in a Democracy?

Michael W. Traugott

At the advent of the modern polling period, there was an extended debate about the role that public opinion polls could play in a democracy. It pitted the pollsters against some academics in a conversation about the contributions that polling could make to an informed debate about policy and the appropriate voice that the public could have in such deliberations. With the passage of time—now more than half a century—there is almost no discussion any longer about whether polls should be used to measure public opinion or that the results should be widely disseminated. The increased number of polling organizations and the advent of polling operations within news organizations have rendered most parts of that debate moot.

Nevertheless, serious questions remain about how the public's voice is being measured, how it is interpreted by those who analyze and report on poll results for public consumption, and whether or not new technology will endanger the collection of representative data by presenting a set of distorted views about what the public thinks or prefers. In a parallel development to the rise in telephone usage (which reduced the cost of conducting polls compared to face-to-face surveys in households in both time and money), the rise of Internet and Web-based polls is luring public pollsters to collect more data faster, often to feed the insatiable appetite of Web sites for new content. But now the problem of representativeness takes on new meaning and raises a different set of concerns.

In this chapter, I trace the origins of modern polling as it relates to recording the public's voice, focusing on the early justifications and rationalizations for legitimizing the technique and the industry. Then

I trace some patterns of organizational development and adaptation that have spread the use of polls and the dissemination of results. And finally I look at problems of contemporary reporting of polls and the strategic use of data that may be distorting the public's voice as reflected in poll results.

Polling as a Representation of the Public's Voice

Since the development of commercial polling by George Gallup and others in the 1930s, proponents have argued that the technique is an ideal forum for expression of the public's sentiment outside the context of elections.[1] Archibald Crossley, writing just after Gallup successfully challenged the *Literary Digest* in projecting the outcome of the 1936 presidential election, viewed the public opinion poll as a way to correct for "false presentations of public opinion" and as "the long-sought key to 'Government by the people.'"[2] Gallup and Rae described public opinion as: "the reserve force in democratic politics [that] can play its part only if the common run of people are continually encouraged to take an interest in the broad lines of public policy, in their own opinions, and in those of their fellows, and if clear channels exist through which these opinions can become known."[3]

These pioneers claimed that polls had an important role to play because elections in the United States occurred systematically but infrequently. There could be issues that politicians avoided or never discussed during campaigns, or certain issues that arose during a presidency or legislative session that could not have been previously discussed because no one knew they would arise. Measurements of public opinion about the U.S. government's responses to the attacks on 11 September 2001 or the disclosures about Enron's business practices and its political contributions are more recent examples of such issues. Polls present an opportunity for citizens to express their opinions and preferences on these matters when the ballot box is not available to them. And the broad dissemination of results keeps the population informed about other citizens' views on important issues of the day.[4]

There have always been critics of the development of public polling. Blumer was one of the earliest; he railed in his 1948 presidential address to the American Sociological Association against the simple aggregation of attitudes as a measurement artifact without any theoretical basis.[5] Ginsberg is a more contemporary critic who is concerned about the ways that the act of polling has transformed the meaning of "public opinion." He describes the measurement of opinions as "externally subsidized" by polling agencies that formulate questions and field surveys on their own schedule rather than as a voluntary form of expression precipitated by serious political concerns. This has also resulted in a transformation of political expression "from a behavioral to an attitudinal phenomenon." And the very act of polling organizations formulating survey questions changes opinion from "a spontaneous assertion to a constrained response."[6]

An important consequence of the trend to increased polling, in his view, is the promotion of the "governance of opinion" rather than "government by opinion."[7] This tendency is exacerbated by the problems that journalists have in reporting public opinion accurately, a result of inadequate methodological training and a lack of familiarity with important public opinion concepts and models. Journalists are also handicapped by the strategic behavior of some groups in misrepresenting the current state of opinion on issues of particular concern to them.[8]

These concerns are also important because government has increasingly adopted the position that the public should be routinely consulted on important issues of the day. Federal agencies require impact assessments of major projects they have authorized, often conducted through polls and surveys. Legislators assess the potential consequences of likely legislation or policy changes through surveys of constituents or through the representation of public opinion in the form of the testimony of others presented before committee hearings.[9] In all of these ways, the argument goes, public opinion has become more accessible but less meaningful, in the sense that it is too easily available through contemporary telephone survey methods or data collected on the Web, but its measurement is often devoid of the forethought and lacking the intensity that characterize reasoned deliberation about politics.

Through these various mechanisms, the assessment of public opinion takes place under an operational assumption of the simple aggregation of attitudes and preferences through the mechanism of polls. For example, the typical poll-based news story pays little attention to the weight of the views of politically active citizens compared to those who are inactive, or to those who feel strongly about the issue at hand as opposed to those who have weakly held or previously nonexistent views on the topic. As Blumer said in his presidential address, "[I]n the process of forming public opinion, individuals are not alike in influence nor are groups that are equal numerically in membership alike in influence."[10] In virtually every contemporary case, the aggregation of measured attitudes to "public opinion" is treated as another element in a calculus of effects or consequences, often set against the views of organized interest groups or acknowledged experts in the area. And its impact is certified and amplified by the very attention that politicians give to the data.

Public Attention to Polls

Even though their evidence is sporadic and episodic, public opinion researchers have been interested in how the public reacts to polls ever since the method came into widespread use. In 1944, Goldman conducted the first national "poll on polls" and showed awareness was widespread and evaluations were generally positive. In his survey, he reported that at least 56% of the respondents knew about polls at the time of his survey; and about one in four respondents followed poll results either "regularly" (9%) or "occasionally" (19%). His results also indicated that the public was generally confident that polls had a positive impact on politics.[11]

There is about a thirty-five-year gap between Goldman's study and subsequent measurements of public opinion on these issues; but questions about public attention to polls have become a regular item for measurement since then, especially in presidential election years. A review of survey databases maintained by the Roper Center and Institute for Research in the Social Sciences at the University of North Carolina provides further documentation of these measures of the public's exposure and attention to poll results. It suggests three broad trends: attention has been increasing over time, most of the questions have been asked in presidential election years, and attention tends to be higher in such periods than at other times.

By 1985, one-quarter of those surveyed indicated that they "regularly" paid attention to polls; this increased to 31% in 1996, more than three times the level in Goldman's survey. When the question was phrased in terms of attention to "election polls" in election-year surveys, two-thirds or more of survey respondents indicated that they had seen them. In a 1988 Gallup survey, 76% of respondents in a national sample indicated they had "heard or read about polls that are predicting who is currently leading in the race for President," and Lavrakas, Holley, and Miller reported that 71% of their 1988 sample had a similar awareness in that campaign.[12] Equivalent levels of attention to presidential polls were measured in a number of local surveys during this same time period as well.[13]

There have been other measures of attention and exposure to polls, most of which have only been asked in the last twenty-five years. For example, a 1976 Harris survey asked respondents whether they read Gallup poll results in newspapers. Even though the focus was specifically on Gallup surveys, one in six respondents (16%) answered that they read Gallup poll results in newspapers "very often." Frequent attention to polls or poll-based coverage is not equivalent to interest in such information. While more than 70% of Americans were aware of poll results in election years, their interest in poll information was not necessarily as high. In their 1988 survey, Lavrakas, Holley, and Miller found that only 28% of the sample indicated that they were either "very interested" or "quite interested" in the results of the opinion polls that were conducted on the Bush-Dukakis race. Three in ten respondents (31%) were "not at all interested," and 41% were only "somewhat interested."[14]

A secondary analysis of a 1996 Gallup poll containing information about public attitudes toward polling highlighted the relative contribution of methodological knowledge on assessments of polls, suggesting that public confidence in polls is, and remains, high.[15] The public is attentive to polls, especially in election years, even if they do not have a strong a priori interest in them. This analysis suggests that the public is receptive to polls reported in the news but may not be actively interested in searching out such information.

The Two Dimensions of Public Interest in Polls

A recent examination of public attitudes about polls and polling revealed the multidimensional nature of the public's interest.[16] A factor analysis of a 1988 national survey produced one attitudinal dimension that measured the public's interest in polls as a way of keeping informed about what other citizens are thinking—that was relatively independent of a second dimension that measured attitudes about how much attention the government should pay to polls when formulating policy. Building upon the theoretical antecedents of Goyder[17] and Dran and Hildreth,[18] two scales were constructed through a factor analysis of several items measuring different aspects of these two dimensions.

Looking at individual items, the survey revealed that there was a high level of interest in media polling. Two out of three respondents (65%) felt that polls conducted by news organizations are a "good way" to inform readers or viewers. Equivalent proportions agreed that polls are a "good way" to learn what other people are thinking (68%) and that a poll is an "opportunity for the silent majority to express their opinions" (62%). About half (51%) felt that "people in government pay too much attention to opinion polls when making new policies," while the public was relatively evenly divided over whether opinion polls have "too much" (46%) or "too little" influence (39%) on Washington.

A number of possible explanations for these relationships were explored. Concerns about polling methods and the representativeness of the results they produce are not correlated with each other. However, a significant proportion of respondents believe that pollsters often try to influence their results, and these views are correlated with concerns about attention to the results. A multivariate analysis based upon specific policy areas showed that the most consistent explanation for supporting the consideration of polls in the development of legislation was their perceived accuracy, a much more important predictor of such beliefs than the Government Attention to Polls Scale, the second most important factor. And the most important predictor of accuracy was whether or not the results of the survey conformed to the respondent's own views on the matter.[19] Methodological concerns were not generally associated with a concern about whether elected officials should consider these polls in deciding laws about these issues.

One surprising result from another analysis of this survey was that virtually all of the individual items about government attention to polls were negatively correlated with socioeconomic status.[20] Concerns about the use of polls as a procedure that simply aggregates and transmits public preferences to elected officials are not randomly distributed in society. Individuals with greater political capital are more likely to express reservations about this process. That is to say, respondents with higher levels of education, income, and political knowledge were less likely to believe that polls were "a good thing," measured in these terms. Higher SES respondents were also more likely to believe that polls have too much influence in Washington and that the government pays too much attention to polls. These negative relationships raise interesting questions about the linkages between the respondents' own status and views and those of others. They also suggest some level of concern about the weight that others' views are given in policy deliberations. This reflects a kind of stratification in society where political elites are more concerned about broad-scale representation than citizens with lower levels of education, income, or political knowledge.

What does the public know about polling methods?

The methods used to collect data have an obvious impact on resulting data quality. Therefore, knowledge of polling methodology should be related to assessments of data quality. Some of those actively engaged in the public opinion business and concerned about the quality of data collection and analysis have promulgated standards to ensure that acceptable and appropriate methods are employed for collecting data and that these procedures are fully disclosed. Both the American Association for Public Opinion Research (AAPOR) and the National Council of Public Polls (NCPP) have established standards for the disclosure of the methodological details of how a specific poll was conducted when its results are reported. The purpose of these standards is to ensure that reports of public opinion findings provide a knowledgeable consumer with enough information to make a critical assessment of quality.

News organizations have increased their reporting of some kinds of methodological information, including descriptions of the design and implementation of the sample, sample size, margin of error, dates of fieldwork, and information about question wordings and order. But this has not increased public knowledge of how these methods work or what their impact on resulting data might be, at least in terms of survey measures of what the public knows. The lack of a relationship between the public's knowledge about polling practices and the assessment of a specific set of results reflects a common problem in survey measurement. When asked general questions about their understanding of survey methods, about six in ten citizens say they "know how public opinion polls work." But when asked about either the details of methods like sampling, their inherent belief in sampling principles, or about how and why data are used, knowledge levels are quite low, and indications of suspicion about polling methods appear.

For example, when asked whether pollsters interview "typical, representative people or they get mostly unusual, nontypical or even oddball types of people," 80% of respondents to a 1985 Roper survey indicated "typical." Yet when they are asked whether "a sample of 1500 to 2000 people can accurately reflect the views of a nation's population," a majority (between 56% and 68%) said it cannot. In a 1995 study for the Council for Marketing and Opinion Research (CMOR), O'Neil reported that the respondents were evenly divided on a statement "I don't understand how interviewing about 500 to 1000 people can tell how the public feels about an issue" (47% agreeing and 50% disagreeing).[21] The 1998 Michigan survey included assessments of the respondents' knowledge of survey methodology; again, 80% of the survey respondents said they did not think it was possible for a sample of 1,500 or 2,000 people to accurately reflect the views of the nation's population, while only 15% said it was.

A second methodological concept that is an essential part of the AAPOR and NCPP disclosure standards is the "margin of error," the imprecision of poll-based estimates that is simply due to chance and is associated with sample size. In a 1987 Roper poll, one-quarter said they found such information in a news story "useful," but 48% said they were not sure of the meaning of the term. Lavrakas, Holley, and Miller asked a national sample how well they understood the meaning of the "margin of error." One-third (33%) said "completely," and 36% said "somewhat." However, when they administered an experimental test of detailed knowledge of the concept, they concluded that such knowledge was low and "many people simply 'guessed' that the hypothetical poll was not accurate enough."[22] In a different form of knowledge test in the Roper poll, only 16% of respondents selected one of four alternatives that correctly reflected the concept. And in the 1998 Michigan survey, only one-third of the respondents indicated they understood "completely" what the concept of the "margin of error" is, while 41% said they understood it "somewhat," 14% "only a little," and 12% "not at all."

These findings suggest that the public's detailed knowledge of polling methods remains limited, despite an increase in the inclusion of some methodological details when polls are reported. This is not surprising, since the information news organizations report is likely to contain the less technical aspects of methodology, and this is not the kind of information that ordinary citizens can be expected to learn through informal exposure. These low levels of knowledge are troubling, however, because a sound foundation of familiarity with polling concepts can be seen as the key to developing the public's critical, analytical, and interpretive skills.

The Impact of Methodology on Measurements of Public Opinion

The range of inadequate data collection techniques is quite wide, even if not employed often. Most commonly, it includes data collected from biased or unrepresentative samples as well as deliberate attempts to sway opinions through the use of biased question wordings or order. Examples of the former category are various forms of biased, nonprobability samples (known as SLOP, or "self-selected listener opinion polls," and CRAP, "computerized response audience polls"), or the representation of the views of participants in small focus groups as if they were the attitudes of the general public.[23] While biased or unrepresentative sampling is usually linked to problems of attitudinal measurement, it has also been linked to problems associated with the networks' calls of the "winner" of the first presidential debate in the

2000 presidential campaign.[24] Postdebate polls based upon standard data collection methods showed Gore as the "winner," while Web-based polls with volunteer samples suggested that Bush had "won." These diverging results can be explained by concerted Republican efforts to overload certain Web sites with volunteer respondents from their party.

Under some circumstances there are also structural problems with the collection of opinions, deriving from other timesaving necessities and conventions of public pollsters. Most public polling data are collected through the use of forced choice (closed-ended) questions in which the respondent is offered only two alternatives, not counting a possible option to express "no opinion." While adequate pretesting of questionnaires goes a long way toward insuring that such questions are balanced and cast in terms of the views that most respondents hold, they nevertheless constrain the ways that some respondents can offer their opinions.

One difficulty with forced choice questions is that the respondent must answer in the frame that the polling organization offers. These forced choices may reflect the division of preferences among elites (for example, in terms of their assessments of feasible policy alternatives), but they also may constrain the public's ability to express their true range of preferences. And such limited choices also foster the notion reflected in a significant proportion of general news reporting that the world is a binary place where political leaders and institutions typically face stark choices cast in black-and-white terms.

It is well known that the structure of closed-ended questions and the response options that are offered to respondents may have a strong impact on the resulting distribution of answers.[25] The effect of more or less strongly worded alternatives, particularly with regard to possible government actions, has been demonstrated in an often-replicated series of questions using the "forbid/allow" alternatives.[26] Krosnick produced experimental results that showed how question wording and response alternatives could affect the measurement of popular opinion about civil litigation reform.[27] He replicated a Harris survey using question forms worded with the four "acceptable" alternatives; a second set of response options of "strongly favor," "somewhat favor," "favor a little," and "not favor at all;" and a third set of response options of "strongly support," "somewhat support," "support a little," and "not support at all." In each case the proportion that found a given reform "acceptable" was greater than those who said they "supported" it.

Is the public influenced by polls?

The dissemination of public opinion data clearly has an impact on subsequent opinion and behavior. While many public pollsters are reluctant to acknowledge this fact, there is growing evidence from academic studies that knowledge of what others think or believe—or how those opinions are changing—has an effect on an individual's opinions and behavior.[28] These impacts are not necessarily negative, as there is usually a more positive version of the same phenomenon; but they are present nevertheless. For example, pre-election polls showing that one candidate has a considerable lead over another may have a depressing effect on turnout; but equivalent information showing that the race is too close to call may stimulate voter participation.

One area in which the impact of the exposure to poll results is most often contested is in research on "bandwagon" and "underdog" effects. The propensity of voters to support a candidate who is ahead or behind is fostered by the publication of poll results that show his or her relative standing. Research in this area has been often hindered by a number of factors, including cross-sectional survey designs that constrained demonstrations of causality as well as the fact that these two effects could be countervailing in the same sample or study. But recent experimental evidence, including that embedded in surveys themselves, clearly suggests that poll results can produce these effects.[29]

There is also research that indicates there is a relationship between the format of news stories and the inclusion of methodological details on the credibility and believability of poll results among those exposed to such content. This research is decidedly mixed because of differences in experimental subjects and stimulus materials, as well as differences in conceptualization of what elements are most relevant to making such assessments. For example, Salwen conducted experiments with undergraduate students and found that the reporting of probability sampling methods was positively correlated with assessments of trustworthiness, expertise, and objectivity, even though such factors as sponsorship and source of the data were not.[30] But Mosier and Ahlgren, in a study of the effects of exposure to "precision," "pseudo-precision," and "traditional" stimulus articles with a set of 275 subjects from the Minnesota military, found no relationship between mode or style of reporting and three dimensions of credibility, measured as accuracy, trustworthiness, and believability.[31]

Journalists and the Reporting of Public Opinion

In general, the increased use of polls has been a positive trend, although some improvements in the use of such data in the news are needed, especially in the coverage of political campaigns.[32] One problem is that most journalists are not well trained to deal with public opinion on a systematic basis because it is not a formal part of their training, is not related to their normal career development, or is not a regular kind of "beat" on which they could even informally develop the necessary expertise. So, at the same time that journalists have a critical intermediary role to play as conveyors of public opinion, they are often ill prepared for the task. This makes most of them uncritical consumers of public opinion data—sometimes prone to errors and susceptible to the manipulation of unscrupulous information providers.

The role of these elites as intermediaries for transmitting public opinion information to a mass audience is critical, because the general public operates essentially on faith that the information that they read or view or hear is accurate and reliable. At the same time that people have a strong interest in what their fellow citizens think about important issues of the day—or even about minor elements of current events—they are by and large completely ignorant of the details of polling methodology. When they are told what "Americans think" on a certain issue, they accept this statement as fact, because they do not have the skills to dissect and evaluate the information in order to form an independent judgment about its reliability and validity, and they have few places to turn for such guidance.[33]

The significance of the role of journalists is highlighted by the degree to which the public is interested in information about public opinion and blindly relies on the media as a source for it. The way that polling methodology is reported in the media is important, because most citizens receive no formal training in sampling, questionnaire design, statistical analysis, or the like. These are not topics covered in the high school curriculum, and even college students would have to search for relevant courses.

Problems of Reporting on Public Opinion: Dealing with Change

Journalists frequently have a problem interpreting survey results when they involve the description of change. One reason is that they cannot distinguish between different types and causes of "change." Some are methodological artifacts of measurement or differences in the conceptualization of change. Others come from aggregation effects that make opinions appear to be more stable than they really are because of counterbalancing trends. Some reports suggest that everyone has changed a little, when in fact the change has been localized in specific subgroups in the population. And sometimes the lack of change in the entire sample masks significant but compensating changes in subgroups.

A common source of error in describing opinion change is the "cross sectional fallacy" in which comparisons are made in the distribution of opinions derived from asking the same question of independent samples drawn from the same population at two different points in time. The aggregate differences are assumed to represent all of the change that has taken place among the individuals in the population being sampled. If 40% of the sample supported Policy A in the first survey and 60% supported the policy in the second survey, a twenty-percentage-point shift is often described as having taken place. Any such comparison between two independent samples, holding other potential sources of error constant, almost certainly underestimates the total amount of shifting opinion. Some people who supported the policy in the first survey may subsequently have opposed it or become undecided; and there may have been offsetting shifts among those who initially opposed the policy. The true assessment of changes in opinion can only be made through the use of panel designs, in which the same respondents are asked the same questions at two or more points in time. Then their responses in the earlier survey can be compared to their later responses, and the full extent of shifting among all response alternatives can be seen.

These problems of reporting on change also occur in campaign reporting, especially when "tracking polls" that measure the "horse race" between candidates is the focal point. Survey research has become an integral part of the reporting of American electoral politics. The essence of politics in general, and campaigns in particular, is a dynamic process strategically organized to produce change. Candidates spend large amounts of money on voter research so that they can develop and evaluate their campaign strategies. Pollsters who take repeated measures of public opinion are expecting change, and this is one of the central features of campaigns that make them newsworthy. And media organizations take the public pulse frequently in order to report on the standing of the candidates, the success of their strategies, and the dynamics of the campaign.

During the campaign, reporters often compare the results of surveys that were conducted by different organizations at different points in time. This can present problems for inferring and explaining change. These issues were especially prevalent in the reporting of the tracking polls in the 2000 presidential election.[34] In a very competitive race, there were more tracking polls than ever. Not only were several polling organizations experimenting with methodological techniques for estimating "likely voters," but they also changed their sample sizes as Election Day neared. And some organizations, especially Gallup, produced a more volatile series of estimates from their tracking polls than others. This made the reporting of the changing fortunes of the candidates extremely difficult. Even though the election outcome was a statistical dead heat in sampling terms, the majority of the final pre-election polls suggested that Bush would win the popular vote in a close race. The fact that Gore actually won the popular vote raises new questions about the meaning of an "accurate" estimate, as well as the ability of the tracking polls to pick up late campaign shifts.

Problems of Reporting on Public Opinion: Dealing with Interest Groups' Data

Most of the poll-based reporting about politics, in the United States and elsewhere, consists of stories organized around surveys that news organizations commission or conduct. However, it is increasingly the case that stories are offered to news organizations by interest groups or individuals because they believe that public consumption of information they want disseminated will be enhanced by the credibility of an independent source like a newspaper or network evening news show. When such stories are "shopped around" to news organizations, the availability of an organization's polling data related to the content may increase the likelihood that journalists will see the information as newsworthy and run the story.

Two recent examples of this phenomenon illustrate the difficulties of relying on interest group data. In the first, reporters were up against a concerted effort by a group of strategic politicians and their paid consultants when they had to deal with with the Republican Party's development of the Contract with America, an organizing device for their 1994 congressional campaign.[35] Republican officials and strategists designed the Contract with America as a unifying theme for the fall campaign in an attempt to nationalize their effort to gain control of the U.S. House of Representatives. At the rollout of the Contract with America, they promoted it to journalists with the claim that each of its ten "reforms" was supported by at least 60% of the American public. Although this claim was widely reported in the media across the entire campaign period, it was not true, based upon a subsequent analysis of extant polling data from a number of sources. This episode provides an interesting case study of how political strategists can take advantage of unwary and untrained journalists through alleged or implied but not revealed polling data.

Evaluating the quality of data obtained in polls and surveys presents a special problem for journalists, since their formal training in interpreting these results is generally weak and inadequate. But journalists can learn to search the archived treasure trove of information available on American public opinion from such organizations as the Roper Center and the Interuniversity Consortium for Political and Social Research, as well as from the Web sites of such longitudinal data collections as the American National Election Studies at the University of Michigan or the General Social Survey at the National Opinion Research Center. By using such sources, reporters would not have to be at the mercy of political operatives and strategists such as Frank Luntz and Newt Gingrich in the case of the Contract with America.

These problems might also arise when interest groups testify before Congress. A study of a brief period during a recent congressional session looked at who was invoking "public opinion" and on what empirical basis.[36] This analysis showed that representatives of interest groups reflected only about one-seventh of the witnesses who appeared before committees to testify, but they made half of the references to "public opinion." Moreover, in only 10% of these cases was there an empirical basis for the claim being made. These facts should affect the weight that congressional members and journalists give to such testimony.

Problems of Reporting on Public Opinion: Public Support for Public Policy and Political Leaders

When the results of surveys are "interpreted" for public consumption, a number of difficulties can arise. Reporters who are not trained in the subtleties of the scientific method generally or survey research methods in particular can make relatively innocent errors when they translate scientific findings for popular consumption. This can result in the careless use of terms that have an explicit scientific meaning, such as "caused."

A very recent example of this phenomenon is what occurred reporting on the impact of the Enron disclosures on the political fortunes of the Democratic and Republican Parties. (Frank Newport, editor-in-chief of the Gallup poll, has raised this most forcefully in a Web-based report on the Gallup Web site.)[37] A *New York Times* front-page article on 27 January 2002 had the headline "Poll Finds Enron's Taint Clings More to G.O.P. than Democrats," while a front-page story from *USA Today* on 29 January 2002 based upon a Gallup poll, had the headline "Bush Gets Benefit of Doubt from Public in Latest Poll." What is the public to make of this?

A knowledgeable consumer would see that the difference in headlines was due to variations in question wording and how they were interpreted by the reporters in the respective stories, undoubtedly with the assistance of the pollsters. In the *New York Times* story, based upon a *New York Times*/CBS poll, there was one question that asked which party "had closer ties" to members of Enron. By a 45% to 10% margin, the sample believed the Republican Party did. However, the question in and of itself does not suggest the negative valence captured in the use of the word "tainted."

The Gallup poll, conducted for *USA Today* and CNN, employed six different questions. The pollsters asked separately about the Democrats' and Republicans' involvement with Enron (in terms of illegal and/or unethical behavior), as well as about Enron donations to the Democrats and to George W. Bush's presidential election campaign and whether they would expect special treat treatment in exchange. There was no significant difference between concerns about either unethical behavior on the part of the Democrats or Republicans (in the first two questions), and more concern about Democrats giving special treatment to Enron executives than Bush. The *New York Times*/CBS poll had a similar finding from a different question, but those results were not chosen for the lead of the story. The differences in the interpretation of the consequences of Enron are a matter of data selection and interpretation, as well as the dissimilarities in the questions asked. And they relate as much to how the headlines were written as to the text of the articles themselves.

Conclusions

How does this analysis help us to answer our original question about whether polls give the public a voice in democracy? The potential for polling to fulfill this role is clearly there. It is better to have good polling data that describes what the public thinks about policy or how the public assesses candidates and their campaigns. The "old style" of reporting would have journalists base their assessments of the public's opinions and reactions on interviews with political elites. This clearly leaves something to be desired, especially given the propensity and sophistication of contemporary elites to "spin" such interpretations to their strategic advantage. In these circumstances, polls provide the public with an independent voice that can act as an antidote to elites' interests and frames of issues and policy.

This is an important function, because the public is generally attentive to polls and seems to value the information it receives along multiple dimensions. Some of poll content is admittedly entertainment in that it supports an interest in what other citizens are thinking. But some of the interest is more instrumental in that it reflects the public's understanding of the potential to communicate citizen preferences to elected officials as they contemplate laws and policy. This function may be tempered by a stratified set of views about whose opinions should carry what weight.

This view needs to be moderated, as well, by the fact that the public does not have very much of an independent ability to discriminate "good" data from "bad." Generally, they do not know much about polling methodology and how it might affect data quality, and they cannot interpret methodological details even when they are disclosed. The most important factor contributing to their assessment of accuracy is whether or not the results conform to their own attitudes or positions.

As a result, the public must rely on journalists for various forms of assistance in deconstructing poll results in the news. This is also problematic, however, because journalists are by and large not very well trained to provide such a service. Beyond their lack of methodological sophistication, their job is complicated by two trends. The first is the increase in the strategic attempts of interest groups to invoke public opinion to promote their own agendas. They sometimes do this with distorted or biased data collections that involve unrepresentative samples and/or biased question wordings. The second is the general growth in data of low or dubious quality, such as the collection of "information" from volunteers who visit Web sites rather than scientific data collected with well-written questionnaires used to interview probability samples.

Despite these cautionary notes, it would be wrong to conclude that the current state of polling has not produced the kind of information that the founding fathers of the industry espoused. Many government agencies now require assessments of public opinion as a formal part of their procedures for evaluating policy and projects. Generally, the major polling organizations and the independent polling units in the major news organizations do a good job of collecting data and reporting the results.

But journalists need to be better trained and to receive more and better assistance from professionals because of their critical intermediary role.[38] They need to act as gatekeepers and vet poll data more thoroughly before writing stories based upon them. This probably means that they need to discard more data than they do currently because of inferior or inadequate methodology or suspicions about the strategic intent of interest group sponsors.

The question is not whether the public should have a voice and polls can appropriately reflect it. The question is whether that voice, as reflected in polling data, is appropriately broadcast through the media. Polls can make an important contribution to democracy when they actually do reflect the public's voice. But they can be a disservice when they don't.

Notes

1. A brief treatment of these developments can be found in Cantril, *Opinion Connection*, while an extended discussion can be found in Converse, "Changing Conceptions."

2. Crossley, "Straw Polls in 1936," p. 35.

3. Gallup and Rae, *Pulse of Democracy*, p. 127.

4. The most recent extreme form of blind faith in such data can be found on Dick Morris's Web site, <www.vote.com>, which is also the title of his new book. He collects opinions without any regard for their representativeness and forwards them to "significant decision makers" such as the president and members of Congress..

5. Blumer, "Public Opinion and Public Opinion Polling."

6. Ginsburg, "How Polling Transforms Public Opinion," p. 275.

7. Ibid., p. 293.

8. Traugott, "The Role of the Mass Media"; Traugott and Powers, "Did Public Opinion Support the Contract with America?."

9. Traugott, "The Invocation of Public Opinion in Congress."

10. Blumer, "Public Opinion and Public Opinion Polling," p. 545.

11. Goldman, "Poll on the Polls."

12. Lavrakas, Holley, and Miller, "Public Reactions to Polling."

13. See Goyder, "Surveys on Surveys," and Dran and Hildreth, "What the Public Thinks," as examples of such studies.

14. Lavrakas, Holley, and Miller, "Public Reactions to Polling."

15. Traugott and Kang, "Public Attention to Polls."

16. Kang et al., "Public Interest in Polling."

17. Goyder, "Surveys on Surveys."

18. Dran and Hildreth, "What the Public Thinks."

19. Presser et al., "How Do People Decide."

20. Traugott, "The Nature of a Belief."

21. O'Neal, "Study for the Council for Marketing and Opinion Research."

22. Lavrakas, Holley, and Miller, "Public Reactions to Polling," p. 163.

23. In the 2000 presidential campaign, AAPOR issued timely press releases about the networks' use of polls and poll-like procedures such as focus groups. One of these releases addressed the inappropriate use of focus groups in key primary states like Florida to generalize to the primary electorate across the country. Examples of such press releases can be found at <http://www.aapor.org/press/focus.html>, visited on 15 February 2002.

24. Traugott, "Assessing Poll Performance."

25. Converse and Presser, *Survey Questions*.

26. Schuman and Presser, *Questions and Answers in Attitude Surveys*; Hippler and Schwarz, "'No-Opinion' Filters."

27. Krosnick, "Question Wording and Reports of Survey Results."

28. Traugott, "The Impact of Media Polls"; Price and Oshagan, "Social Psychological Perspectives on Public Opinion."

29. Lavrakas, Holley, and Miller, "Public Reactions to Polling."

30. Salwen, "The Reporting of Public Opinion Polls during Presidential Years."

31. Mosier and Ahlgren, "Credibility of Precision Journalism."

32. Gawiser and Witt, *Journalist's Guide to Public Opinion Polls*; Lavrakas, Holley, and Miller, "Public Reactions to Polling"; Lavrakas, Traugott, and Miller, *Presidential Polls and the News Media*; Mitofsky, "How Pollsters and Reporters"; Worcester, "Journalist's Guide."

33. Traugott and Lavrakas, *Voter's Guide*.

34. Traugott, "Assessing Poll Performance."

35. Traugott and Powers, "Did Public Opinion Support the Contract with America?."

36. Traugott, "The Invocation of Public Opinion in Congress."

37. The full discussion can be found at <https://www.gallup.com/poll/FromtheEd/ed0202.asp>, viewed on 15 February 2002.

38. Traugott, "Asessing Poll Performance."

6

When Push Comes to Shove: Push Polling and the Manipulation of Public Opinion

Matthew J. Streb
and
Susan H. Pinkus

With each passing election cycle, polling has become a more integral part of candidates' campaigns and has played an increased role in the media's reporting of voting patterns. As the importance of polling to candidates, the media, and researchers increases, citizens must be aware of the quality of the polls being conducted. Many organizations are—by intent—failing to run scientific, reliable polls. This chapter focuses on one of the more devious, fraudulent, and increasingly popular ways of polling: push polling. We begin by explaining what push polling is, and then discuss the increased prominence of push polls and the attempts of polling organizations and legislatures to limit their use. We go on to mention several other polling practices that citizens must be aware of, and we close by arguing that these types of polls undermine a healthy democracy by reporting inaccurate information and raising cynicism about polls and politics in general.

What Is a Push Poll?

The term "push poll" is actually inaccurate, because a push poll is not a poll at all. The NCPP, a watchdog organization for the polling industry, referred to push polls as "masquerading as legitimate political polling," when in fact "they are political telemarketing."[1] In a push poll, respondents are presented with hypothetical, sometimes blatantly false information under the guise of legitimate survey research.

Pollsters who conduct push polls are using unethical and unfair tactics to boost their candidate in the eyes of the voters or to create a negative impression of the opponent. They are using a deceitful method to "push" a person towards their candidate and away from a candidate that the respondent might have initially supported.

The following is an example of a push poll mentioned in the *Sarasota Herald Tribune*.[2]

> Caller: Are you planning to vote in the Smith-Jones race for senate?
>
> You: Yes.
>
> Caller: And whom do you plan to vote for?
>
> You: Jones.
>
> Caller: Tell me if your vote would be affected definitely, possibly or not at all if you knew that Jones had been charged with passing bad checks.
>
> You: Uh, possibly.
>
> Caller: And, if you knew that Jones had been arrested for drunken driving? Would that affect your vote definitely, possibly or not at all?
>
> You: Oh, definitely.
>
> Caller: Thank you very much. We appreciate you taking the time to help us.

If you had said you were going to vote for Smith, the caller would have thanked you and hung up without asking any other questions.

As you can see from the phone call, the interviewer did not say Jones was charged with kiting checks or was even arrested for drunk driving. They were hypothetical questions, but clearly left the impression that Jones actually did these things. The sponsor of this poll was hoping that the respondent believed that Jones had a problem. The callers even thanked the respondent for participating, making it seem like a legitimate poll.

Push polls have several distinct features that might indicate to a respondent that they are participating in one. In a letter decrying the use of push polls, Bill McInturff, a partner at Public Opinion Strategies, a Republican polling/consulting firm, distinguished between push polling and legitimate polling. McInturff wrote:

> The rapid rise in the use of "push polling" as a campaign tactic has lead to significant confusion between advocacy polling and legitimate survey research. The differences between push polling and survey research could not be more dramatic:

—Every survey research firm opens its interviews by providing the name of the survey firm or the telephone research center conducting the interviews. Most push polls provide no name of a sponsoring organization.
—Survey research firms only interview a limited sample of people that attempts to mirror the entire population being studied. Push polls contact thousands of people per hour with the objective of reaching sometimes hundreds of thousands.
—Survey research firms conduct interviews of between five minutes for even the shortest of tracking questionnaires to over 35 minutes for a major benchmark study. Push polls are generally designed to be 30 to 60 seconds long.
—Survey research firms use different questionnaire design techniques to assess how voters will respond to new information about your candidate and the opponent. Push polls are designed solely as a persuasion vehicle.[3]

Since push poll calls are quite brief and data usually is not collected, far more people can be reached. Unlike a scientific poll where the pollster must be concerned with obtaining a representative sample, push polling organizations want to reach as many voters as possible and are not concerned with sample bias. The object is to get negative information to as many people as quickly as possible. Therefore, most push polls are conducted in the last two weeks of a campaign, when it will most likely have the greatest impact and opposing campaigns have less time to react. The final days of the campaign are when candidates are the most vulnerable to any negative revelations about them and when candidates who are victims of this type of polling may not be able to answer the charges. It is also less likely that the push poll will be exposed before the election. Push polling is normally well below anyone's radar unless the opposing side was called and heard the question or someone called the opposing candidate to complain. Even then, because of the anonymity of the calls, it is difficult to pin down just who is responsible for conducting the push poll.

Also, it is sometimes difficult to determine if a question is a push poll question or a legitimate question that is asked about a candidate by a reputable polling firm. There is a fine line between the two. Many campaigns and media polling organizations use questions to get at whether a candidate's belief about an issue or behavior has an effect on how the respondent will vote. Polling is extremely important for creating a campaign strategy and understanding the dynamics of the race. For polls to provide meaningful information, pollsters must be able to ask about negative information, as long as the question is asked in an unbiased way. An example of a legitimate question designed to obtain information about voting intention can be found in a *Los Angeles Times* poll regarding the March 2002 California Republican primary for governor. The committee to support the incumbent governor, Gray Davis, ran a television ad showing Richard Riordan, one of the Republican candidates, referring to abortion as murder. The polling firms in the state wanted to test the public's reaction to this negative advertisement. A February 2002 *Los Angeles Times* poll asked this question about Riordan's position on abortion:[4]

> As you may know, Gray Davis' campaign has been running ads showing Richard Riordan being interviewed by a reporter in the early 1990's about his views on abortion. In the ad, Riordan says that he considers abortion to be murder. However, in spite of his beliefs about abortion, Riordan says he strongly believes in a woman's right to choose. Based on what you just heard, does that make you more likely to vote for Riordan for governor, or less likely, or does that not affect your vote one way or the other?[5]

Even though this question includes a negative statement, it is not a push poll question. It gives voters both sides of the story: (1) Riordan did say abortion was murder, but (2) in spite of this statement, he believes in a woman's right to choose. It was a question that was information-based and fair to the candidate. Also, this was part of a series of questions about all the candidates running for governor. It was question 56 in a poll that lasted about twenty minutes. In addition, the interviewer stated his name and mentioned that it was a *Los Angeles Times* poll. Demographics were asked at the end of the survey. Because data is rarely collected in a push poll, respondents usually are not asked demographic questions, such as age, race, education, and income.

The rise of push polling has created several major problems. First, legitimate negative polling conducted by a candidate is often labeled by his/her opponent as push polling. As we stated, candidates must be able to ask questions about their opponents for research purposes. Also, candidates and the media often fail to distinguish between push polling and persuasion calling. Pollsters generally agree that persuasion calling is acceptable, because it is a form of campaigning that does not disguise itself as a legitimate poll. As with push polls, the object of persuasion calling is to reach as many people as possible by using a short, prepared script disseminating negative information about the opponent. Unlike push polling, however, persuasion calling clearly identifies who is paying for the phone call, and it is not done under the guise of a poll.[6]

More importantly, however, the use of push polling damages the electoral process. According to the NCPP, "[Push polls] injure candidates, often without revealing the source of the information. Also, the results of a 'Push Poll,' if released, give a seriously flawed and biased picture of the political situation."[7] In addition, push polls are likely to make citizens more cynical of politics and less willing to trust legitimate survey research. As a result, the NCPP, the Association of Political Consultants (AAPC), and the AAPOR have all released statements strongly condemning the practice of push polling.

The Prominence of Push Polling

Unfortunately, push polling—or at least the alleged use of push polling—has become quite common in elections for all levels of office in the United States, including campaigns for the presidency, Congress, and state legislatures, and even in state initiative campaigns. The use of push polling is also prominent in local elections, because there is normally little media scrutiny, making it easier for push polls to go undetected. As Sabato and Simpson note, push polling has become "the rage" in American campaigns.[8] At a national level, push polls came to the forefront in the 1996 Republican primaries when Bob Dole and Steve Forbes were both accused of financing them. A firm well known for conducting push polls was hired by Dole and called voters in Iowa and New Hampshire asking if they would be more or less likely to support Forbes if they knew that Forbes was pro-choice and backed President Clinton's decision to allow gays in the military. The Forbes campaign asked questions regarding Dole's vote to fund a $6.4 million ski resort in Idaho and an $18.4 million subway for senators to get from their offices to the Capitol.[9]

While the Dole and Forbes campaigns were chastised for their use of push polls, the criticism certainly has not stopped others from conducting questionable polls. Sabato and Simpson interviewed forty-five candidates for Congress in 1994, and almost 80% claimed that push polling had been used against them.[10] Allegations of push polling have been made in high profile races including the 2000 New York

Senate race, the 2001 New York City mayoral campaign, and the 2001 special election in Massachusetts's Ninth Congressional District to replace longtime congressman Joseph Moakley, just to name a few. In all three cases, the candidates accused of push polling adamantly denied any improper polling by their campaigns. These three elections show just how complex and problematic push polling is.

The 2000 New York Senate race, initially between Republican candidate Rudolph Giuliani and Democratic candidate Hillary Rodham Clinton, and then later between Republican nominee Rick Lazio and Clinton, was rife with allegations of push polling. Giuliani first levied a charge against Clinton in February. The former New York mayor was upset because a Democratic polling firm made statements, including: "If elected, Rudy Giuliani said he would vote for Supreme Court judges who are against abortion," followed by the traditional question of whether the person's attitude toward Giuliani changed. While Clinton distanced herself form the poll, Democrats said that calls were made to roughly eight hundred voters, lasted approximately twenty-five minutes, and were used for general research.[11] The small number of people contacted, the relatively long survey, and the fact that it occurred so far in advance of the election are indications that the Democrats may have been polling for legitimate strategy purposes. The Clinton case indicates a major problem with push polls. It is difficult for candidates to conduct legitimate polls to help them devise strategy without the opponent accusing them of push polling. And once again, this is another example of the fine line between legitimate polls and push polls.

Clinton later charged Lazio, her opponent when Giuliani dropped out of the race after being diagnosed with prostate cancer, of engaging in push polling. The New York Republican State Committee made calls to more than five hundred thousand New Yorkers questioning Clinton's support of Israel and tying her to a Mideast terrorism group, a group that, according to the script, practiced "the same kind of terrorism that killed our sailors on the U.S.S. Cole."[12] Republicans asserted that they were not push polling, because they identified that the calls were coming from the party. Instead, Republicans claimed that these were persuasion calls. Again, the problem of identifying a push poll is clear.

In the 2001 New York City mayoral election, the Republican Herman Badillo accused the eventual winner, Michael Bloomberg, of "dirty tricks," including push polling.[13] According to a Badillo supporter, the polling firm Penn, Schoen & Berland, who conducted polls for the Bloomberg campaign, called and asked whom the respondent intended to support. When the man replied "Badillo," the interviewer went through a list of negative statements about Badillo, including his opposition to open admissions for high school graduates at City University of New York and the fact that Badillo had been a Democrat for thirty years.[14] The Bloomberg campaign strongly denied Badillo's charges. Interestingly, when the *New York Times* contacted Penn, Schoen, & Berland, they referred all questions on the controversial poll to the Bloomberg campaign.[15]

The 2001 special election for Massachusetts's Ninth Congressional District was even more heated and surrounded in controversy. Supporters of state senator Stephen F. Lynch, including Lynch's wife, complained about a poll that they had participated in that asked respondents how they felt about Lynch's well-known financial problems and his arrests several years earlier.[16] The script also said that Lynch has a "history of physically threatening people who disagree with him."[17] In addition, the questionnaire had one blatant factual mistake. Respondents were asked whether the fact that opponent Brian A. Joyce had five children and Lynch had none made them feel differently about Lynch. In fact, Lynch has one child.

The controversy surrounding the poll became quite intense as Lynch initially blamed Joyce for being behind the poll. The poll in question was conducted by the Parker Group, which, as is normally the case, denied that the poll was a push poll and refused to provide a list of their clients. Though Joyce was originally charged with financing the poll, it was later discovered that another pollster with ties to state senator Cheryl Jacques, also a candidate for the Ninth District seat, had commissioned the survey. The heat then turned on Jacques, who of course denied involvement. Jacques argued that the survey contained negative information about her as well. The poll asked questions about Jacques's female partner living in a low-cost apartment and the extensive pay raises given to the woman by Jacques when she was an employee for the state senator. All of the candidates, then, seemed to have an "alibi." The only certainty of the situation was that Tony Parker, the head of the Parker Group, and Anna Bennett, the woman who Parker eventually claimed commissioned the poll and who had ties to Emily's List, had been charged with push polling in the past. Parker, in particular, had been tied to push polls on several occasions, including one in which false rape and assault charges were levied against the Alabama candidate for lieutenant governor Steve Windom.[18]

Not everyone was convinced that the poll in question was a push poll. Francis J. Connolly and Charley Manning, both of whom have been involved in Democratic and Republican campaigns, wrote in an op-ed piece in the *Boston Globe* that people too often label polls as push polls when in fact they are not. Connolly and Manning argued that the poll seems to have been a "flawed—but legitimate—political poll."[19] They asserted that almost all political polls use push questions to allow candidates to gauge public opinion and devise strategy. While Connolly and Manning may be correct, the poll conducted in the Ninth District makes reputable pollsters cringe. Because of the length of the survey and the fact that it contained negative information about all of the candidates, one can question whether it was an intentional push poll. However, the sloppiness of the survey (e.g., the false claim about Lynch's family and the fact that some interviewers were mispronouncing his first name as "Stefan") can lead respondents to question the quality and usefulness of survey research.

While discussion of push polling was abundant in the cases just cited, nowhere have push polls received more press coverage than in the 2000 Republican presidential primaries. In a contest that became quite bitter, Senator John McCain argued that George W. Bush's campaign was behind controversial phone calls made to voters in South Carolina. While campaigning, McCain met a woman who said that her fourteen-year-old son had spoken to a survey interviewer who referred to the senator as "a cheat, liar, and a fraud." McCain quickly accused the Bush campaign of being behind the survey. The Bush campaign denied that they were engaging in push polling and released an "advocacy calling" script to the press. The advocacy calls were made to roughly two hundred thousand voters in South Carolina and blamed McCain for the negative tone of the race.[20] Also, the Bush campaign said Voter/Consumer Research conducted a poll for Bush to determine which issues were important to voters in South Carolina. While the Voter/Consumer Research poll did ask several detailed questions, leading many to assert that it was in fact not a push poll, the Bush campaign's claim that the survey was conducted for research purposes is debatable. The following questions from the Voter/Consumer Research survey were provided to the *New York Times* by the Bush campaign.

> Q: Here are three points people have made about John McCain's position on taxes. Please tell me for each of these whether you strongly approve, somewhat approve, somewhat disapprove, or strongly disapprove.
>
> A) John McCain's plan does not cut tax rates for 71% of all taxpayers.
>
> B) John McCain's plan will increase taxes on charitable contributions to churches, colleges, and charities by $20 billion.

C) John McCain says he never voted for a tax increase, but he wrote legislation that proposed the largest tax increase in United States history.

Q: Here are some points regarding John McCain's record on campaign finance reform. Again please tell me whether you strongly approve, somewhat approve, somewhat disapprove, or strongly disapprove.

A) He has written legislation that would use taxpayer dollars to pay for political campaigns.

B) He was reprimanded by the Senate Ethics Committee for intervening with the federal regulators who were investigating Charles Keating, one of his campaign contributors who went to jail for bank fraud in the Savings and Loan scandal.

Q: John McCain calls the campaign finance system corrupt, but as chairman of the Senate Commerce Committee, he raises money and travels on private jets of corporations with legislative proposals before his committee. In view of this are you much more likely to vote for him, somewhat more likely to vote for him, somewhat more likely to vote against him or much more likely to vote against him?

Q: John McCain's campaign finance proposals would give labor unions and the media a bigger influence on the outcome of elections. Again, in view of this are you much more likely to vote for him, somewhat more likely to vote for him, somewhat more likely to vote against him or much more likely to vote against him?[21]

In response to the Bush survey, comedian Al Franken suggested that the McCain camp run a similar poll for the Michigan primary. Franken believed that voters should be asked the following question: "We're an independent polling company conducting a survey for Tuesday's primary. If you knew that while John McCain was hanging by his thumbs in a North Vietnamese prison, George W. Bush was throwing a keg party at a Yale secret society that didn't allow Catholics to date Jews, would you be more or less likely to vote for Bush?"[22]

Technically, if one defines push polling as polling containing a few short, pointed questions, the Bush campaign is not guilty. The campaign did ask for demographic data, which a push poll would normally not do. And if the claim of the Bush campaign is true, that only three hundred people were included in the survey, it certainly does not appear to be a classic push poll. The Bush campaign could have found a more efficient way to get negative information about McCain across to voters.

However, one can still question the legitimacy of the survey and the reasons why it was conducted. While the Bush campaign was forthright with the survey and argued it was used for research purposes, the quality of the data that the Bush campaign obtained was likely to provide little helpful information, leading one to suspect their motives. The questions asked were loaded; few people would say they were more likely to approve of McCain because of his involvement in the Keating loan scandal or the fact that his tax cut would fail to apply to a majority of all taxpayers. Perhaps, however, the Bush campaign was trying to measure how intensely voters opposed each statement. If they found, for example, that few respondents were upset about the small percentage of people that qualified for tax cuts (as Bush interpreted McCain's plan), but that many were strongly disenchanted with McCain because of his involvement in the Keating loan scandal, the Bush campaign might decide to drop their attacks on the tax plan and instead focus on the loan scandal. But even if this were the intent, little useful information would be uncovered. As we said, few people were more likely to support McCain because of these probes (even his supporters), and respondents were not given a "neutral" response alternative. A person might not approve of McCain because of his involvement in the loan scandal, but may not care enough for it to affect her rating. It would be difficult for the Bush campaign to ascertain this information without giving the respondent a midpoint alternative. A better alternative would be "How important is McCain's involvement in the Keating loan scandal in determining your vote?"

In fairness to the Bush campaign, questions such as those in their survey are quite common.[23] Whether the survey was "officially" a push poll is not the issue. Certainly, candidates must be able to conduct research on the strengths and weaknesses of both themselves and their opponents. A poll of this nature, though, is questionable because it appears to have been designed as a "long push poll." As in the poll in the Massachusetts Ninth Congressional District race, the survey was poorly constructed and provided little valuable information. While this might simply be a poor use of money by the Bush campaign, polling such as his campaign conducted in South Carolina is still problematic. These polls have the potential to create negative feelings about the political process.

Push polling has extended beyond the boundaries of the United States, although one *Toronto Sun* article referred to push polling as "a controversial U.S. style campaign tactic."[24] In Australia in 2001, the Liberal Party went to court to attempt to stop the Labor Party from calling voters in marginal seats and telling them that the Liberal Party would raise the rate of the GST tax to 15%; the Liberal Party claimed that Labor was push polling.[25] The Labor Party responded that all callers identified themselves as calling on behalf of the party. The court dismissed the case because of lack of evidence.

The preceding examples are interesting, because in each case the candidate or party charged with push polling denied it. Push polls are like racial code words; people are accused of using them all the time, but no one is going to explicitly admit to using them. Some of the earlier examples may indeed not be push polling. Without having access to the script, the sample, and the tabulated results, it is hard for one to tell. Two things emerge as problematic, however. First, whenever candidates are upset with the polling strategies of their opponents, they seem to immediately allege that their opponents are push polling, but do not seem to completely understand exactly what a push poll is. This trend is disconcerting to pollsters, because it provides negative press coverage of polling, which, in turn, could make people question legitimate polls or be less likely to participate in them. Traugott and Kang assert that the media are the best way to make the public aware of push polls and thus limit their effectiveness.[26] For the most part, we agree. Negative media coverage may make a candidate think twice before using push polls, and it has the potential to inform the public about the unethical practice. The problem is complex, though. The media often have difficulty distinguishing between legitimate polling, persuasion calling, and push polling. Because of this, the media normally just report the alleged use of push polls—in some cases when the poll is not a push poll at all. Citizens are not being taught to differentiate between legitimate polling and push polling. Citizens may become skeptical of any poll—even those that are legitimate. Also, it is difficult for the media to take a candidate to task for using push polls if the media cannot determine if the poll is indeed a push poll

Second, even if the previous examples were not classic push polling, the use of this kind of internal polling by candidates is worrisome. Certainly we are not saying that candidates should not be able to poll; polling is essential to understanding how the public feels about issues. We are concerned with the quality of the polling that is being conducted. The Bush poll we mentioned may not be classic push polling, because it asked several questions and only a few hundred respondents were surveyed, but the fact that interviewers are calling respondents, saying that they are conducting a survey, and proceeding to make clearly loaded statements is problematic. As was clear from the newspaper accounts of the Bush survey, many respondents were disgusted by the Bush poll. These polls make it more difficult for legitimate surveys to be conducted.

The Fight against Push Polls

Because of the controversy surrounding push polls and the proliferation of them by both parties, many state legislatures, and even Congress, have tried to pass legislation banning or at least limiting the use of push polls. In 1997, the "Push Poll Disclaimer Act" (H.R. 248) was introduced in the House of Representatives and sent to the House Committee on Government Reform and Oversight. The bill would "require individuals conducting polls by telephone or electronic means to interview individuals on opinions relating to any election for Federal office, to disclose the following information: (1) the individual's identity; (2) the identity of the individual sponsoring the poll or paying the expenses associated with the poll; and (3) if during the interview the individual provides information relating to a candidate for the election, the source of the information (or, if there is no source, a statement to that effect)."[27] However, the bill never made it out of committee. Several similar bills have been introduced in the House, but all have had the same fate as H.R. 248.

State legislatures have had more success passing legislation designed to limit the use of push polls West Virginia has passed one of the most aggressive laws restricting push polls. According to Traugott and Kang, the West Virginia law "limits the use of public opinion polls to the 'gathering, collection, collation, and evaluation of information reflecting public opinion, needs, and preferences as to any candidate, group of candidates, party issue or issues.'"[28] While the West Virginia state legislature should be commended for trying to stop push polling, the law is difficult to enforce. For instance, the Bush survey discussed previously was considered by many to be push polling, but would likely be legal under West Virginia law, since the Bush campaign argued it was for research purposes. As Fox wrote regarding the West Virginia law, "The practical impact of the statute is limited because it lacks objective standards for determining the intent of the poll sponsor."[29] Fox noted that, even with the new law on the books, there were still charges of push polling in the 1996 West Virginia gubernatorial election.

Other states have tried to limit the use of push polls as well. In 1997, Florida passed legislation that required anyone making a telephone call in favor or against a candidate or issue to identify the sponsor of the call. According to Fox,

> The . . . Florida law prohibits telephone callers from misrepresenting an affiliation with a person or existing organization without specific approval, and also prohibits misrepresenting an affiliation with a fictitious organization. In addition, the law requires that a candidate or sponsor of a ballot proposal first approve the calls in writing, unless the call is an independent expenditure, and file the written approval with the qualifying officer. Finally, the law requires persons or organizations making paid telephone calls to individuals in Florida to establish a registered agent for service of process prior to commencing the calls.[30]

The Florida law is interesting, Fox stated, because

> the statutory criteria for defining a push poll are based on specific objective manifestations of the poll sponsor's subjective intent, namely, a maximum sample size of 1000 and average call duration of less than two minutes. The Florida approach provides poll sponsors and pollsters with specific, enforceable guidelines for when a sponsorship disclaimer is required and when it is not.[31]

Several other states, including Nebraska, New Hampshire, Nevada, and Wisconsin, have passed legislation that deals directly or indirectly with push polls.

The statutes limiting push polling or requiring callers to identify themselves raise First Amendment questions. Larry Frankel, executive director of the American Civil Liberties Union of Pennsylvania, testified against a proposed Pennsylvania law that would bans polls that contain "'willfully false, fraudulent, or misleading' innuendo posing as legitimate scientific polling questions."[32] According to Frankel, "The ACLU believes that steps can be taken to combat negative campaigning without putting the government in the role of regulating political speech."[33]

The courts have not reached a consensus on the constitutionality of such statutes. According to Fox, "The general principal [sic] which grows out of most of these cases [dealing with required identification] is that a ban on all anonymous political advertising is probably unconstitutional, but that a more narrowly-drawn statute might pass constitutional muster."[34] In *Talley v. California*, the Supreme Court argued that anonymous publishing is part of the American experience, and it struck down a Los Angeles ordinance requiring an identification disclaimer on any political pamphlet. The Court ruled:

> Anonymous pamphlets, leaflets, brochures and even books have played an important role in the progress of mankind. Persecuted groups and sects from time to time throughout history have been able to criticize oppressive practices and laws either anonymously or not at all. . . .Before the Revolutionary War colonial patriots frequently had to conceal their authorship and distribution of literature that easily could have brought down on them prosecutions by English-controlled courts. . . . Even the Federalist Papers, written in favor of the adoption of our Constitution, were published under fictitious names. It is plain that anonymity has sometimes been assumed for the most constructive purposes.[35]

The *Talley* case does not specifically apply to push polls, however, nor does it discuss purposely false speech or writing.

The Use and Abuse of Other Unscientific Polls

While perhaps most problematic, push polls are not the only polls that should concern the public. Several other forms of questionable polls have emerged. These "pseudo polls" do not conform to the guidelines set forth by the NCPP and the AAPOR because of how the sample of respondents is selected. The major difference between scientific and unscientific polls is who chooses the respondents for the survey. In a scientific poll, the pollster randomly identifies people to be interviewed. In an unscientific poll, the respondents usually "volunteer" their opinions, selecting themselves for the poll. While there are many other aspects of the poll to analyze, such as the methodology of the poll (e.g., sample size, margin of error, dates of the interviews), and the question ordering and wording, one should be quite cautious of polls that allow respondents to self-select themselves into the sample. The following is a brief discussion of several of the "pseudo polls," all of which, unfortunately, are quite prominent today.

Frugging

"Frugging" is simply fund-raising under the guise of research. You may have received mail from charities or political parties asking you to complete a questionnaire and then, at the end of the questionnaire, encouraging you to donate money to help that particular charity or political candidate. Most of the questions are biased, and results are skewed in favor of that group's positions. These are not legitimate polls. If people belong to an organization (i.e., Sierra Club, Amnesty International, the National Rifle Association, or the Democratic/Republican National Committees) they have a proclivity toward a certain mind-set that would skew the results differently than if the American public was interviewed. Only those who are deeply concerned about a particular issue will likely answer (or even receive) the questionnaire; therefore, the results will not represent the general public's views.

Sugging

The same holds true for completing a questionnaire and then at the end having a company try to sell you something; this is known as "sugging"—selling under the guise of research. For example, you might receive a phone call in which you are asked to participate in a survey designed to research music preferences—what kinds of music do you listen to, do you go to concerts, and how many hours a day do you listen to music on the radio or on your stereo? At the end of the survey, you might be asked to buy CDs. This, too, is inaccurate, unreliable polling. Like push polls and "frugging," "sugging" is also problematic because respondents may become cynical of legitimate research surveys.

900 or 800 dial-in surveys

This technique is popular on television. Many of these surveys, when reported on, have disclaimers saying they are not scientific polls. But, unfortunately, these disclaimers seem to lose their way when discussed by other media. The media may pick up the findings of a survey that is not conducted properly, and thus another inaccurate result lives on. A blatant example of this type of "pseudo poll" occurred after a 1980 presidential debate between Jimmy Carter and Ronald Reagan. ABC News asked viewers to call one number if they believed Carter won the debate and another number if they believed Reagan was victorious; each call cost fifty cents. ABC News announced that Reagan had won the debate by a 2–1 margin. "Ideally, Americans would have dismissed this instant poll as foolish and unsound," wrote Asher. "Unfortunately, because it was the first large-scale reaction to the debate to be publicized, the poll and ABC's reporting of it shaped subsequent perceptions of who won the debate."[36]

The reason that ABC's use of the dial-in poll is so egregious is that dial-in polling is self-selective. First, in 900 dial-in polls, a person who wants to take the poll has to pay, which already limits the kinds of people answering the questionnaire; there is likely to be an income bias. Second, it is difficult to determine how many times a person is calling to express his/her view or even if that person is a child or an adult. A group with an agenda could start a phone bank and in the process purposely tie up the lines so that a person with a different point of view would be unable to participate. For example, in a poll on gun control, the NRA could galvanize its membership and have them call more than once to voice their opinion that they are against gun control, while freezing out anyone else from calling in.

The 800 dial-in polls should not be reported for the same reason that 900 dial-in polls should not. Even though the phone call is free, the person calling is likely to have a vested interest in the issue. Again, organizations on one side of an issue or the other could mobilize their people and start a telephone campaign. This procedure does not provide a representative sample of the American public.

Internet polling

Internet polls suffer from similar problems as the dial-in surveys. They receive unrepresentative samples, since many people do not have access to the Internet and not everyone who has access will visit the site conducting the poll. Also, as with dial-in polls, the opportunity to "flood" the results exists. Nowhere is this more apparent than in trial-heat surveys. In the 2000 presidential election, "flooding" of web polls was quite common. Traugott mentions an e-mail, forwarded to him from Gary Langer of ABC, that Jim Nicholson, the former chairmen of the Republican National Committee, had sent to supporters. Nicholson had written:

> Moreover, we are hearing that many liberal left wing groups will be trying to stack the vote in favor of a Democratic candidate by bombarding the various news websites which will be polling immediately following the debate. In addition to watching the debate, you should log on to: <http://www.conn.com/allpolitics> or alternatively go online at: <http://abcnews.go.com/sections/politics/> and express your support for who you think won the debate! The Democrats and their left-wing allies are very good at organizing such guerilla efforts. We are alerting you to give you the opportunity as an individual to be heard as loudly as these liberal special interest groups.[37]

Each of the four polls regarding the debate using probability samples estimated that Gore had performed better, while all three of the Web polls indicated that Bush won the debate.[38]

Political consultant Dick Morris is an ardent advocate of Internet polling. In fact, his Web site, <www.vote.com>, asks people daily questions, and the results are forwarded to elected officials. "In Internet voting it is the people who are the activists and the initiators," writes Morris, "and the politicians who must wait their turn and listen to what the people say."[39] Morris argues that the Internet will get more people participating in the polls, which will allow researchers to do more analysis. Internet polling is an interesting idea, but unlike Morris, we believe its time has not yet come. The Internet is good for certain samples, such as a membership of an organization or students on a college campus, but as far as a national probability sample, it has many inherent problems. The Internet population is lacking in minorities, the elderly, and households with low socioeconomic demographics. Again, one must be quite skeptical of polls that allow people to select themselves into the sample. These polls only tell us what the people who participated in the poll think; they cannot be generalized to the public as a whole.

Morris claims that, while this is true, "polling itself has moved away from being statistically representative of the general population."[40] He continues:

> Political polls that survey everybody are derided as worthless since they make no distinction between those who are registered to vote and those who are not. Even polls of voters are usually dismissed since they do not separate those who are likely to vote from voters who habitually stay home. Increasingly, pollsters don't really bother to measure what everybody thinks. Rather, they want to know what registered voters who are very likely to vote think. It is only their opinions that matter to their clients.[41]

We take issue with Morris's comments. He is probably correct that people who respond on the Internet are more likely to vote. This still does not get around the problem of self-selection. Statistical theory allows us to determine the poll's margin of error. The margin of error allows pollsters to say that the true value of the population falls somewhere around the value of the sample. For example, a simple random sample—where everyone in the population has an equal chance of being chosen—of 1,500 respondents has a margin of error of +/- 2.5. This means that if the poll results indicate that 75% of the people approve of President Bush's handling of the terrorism crisis, the real percentage is anywhere between 72.5% and 77.5%. Without using probability sampling, we have no idea where the true value falls. With Internet polling, it is quite plausible that an overwhelming number of respondents were Republicans, which caused Bush's popularity to be so high in our hypothetical example. Morris claims that larger numbers of respondents make it easier to do more analysis. While pollsters would always love a larger number of respondents, it is the strength of the design of the survey sample that is most important, not the number of respondents. The infamous *Literary Digest* poll that predicted Alf Landon would defeat Franklin Roosevelt in the 1936 presidential election had more than two million responses. The poll was wrong because the sample was biased; the large number of respondents in the survey still provided inaccurate information.

Finally, Morris argues that Internet polling is advantageous because it shows the opinions of people who feel deeply about an issue. But, unfortunately, it is the strength of "self-selective" respondents, which disproportionately excludes certain demographic groups, that Internet polling reports on. This self-selection provides an inaccurate picture of public opinion. Certainly it is important to understand strength of preference, but this can easily be obtained in a probability sample by asking a strength of preference question.

Though we are quite critical of Morris's use of the Internet, we believe the Internet has the potential to be a great resource to pollsters, *assuming they use a probability sample and people do not select themselves into the sample*. It is important to remember that it was not long ago that telephone interviewing—the most common interviewing technique today—was frowned upon because of low penetration in households. As more households have Internet access, it is likely that polling organizations will use the Internet more and the telephone less.

The Threat to a Democratic Society

The problem with unscientific or unethical polling, such as Internet polls and push polls, is that they undermine the public's faith in legitimate polling. Polls serve an important purpose in a democratic society. In a representative democracy, people should have an influence over policy. Polls are one way to allow the people to have a voice and they allow politicians to measure that voice. In addition, polling is important for any campaign to develop strategy.

Polls that allow the respondent to select themselves into the sample are problematic because they tell us very little, yet people may think that the results of those polls are quite accurate of the general population's beliefs. The media, as was the case in the ABC News poll on the 1980 presidential debate, often do not or cannot differentiate between good and bad polls. They report the polls as fact when, in reality, these kinds of pseudo polls do not represent what the American public think. Instead, they perpetuate what unethical pollsters want the public to think by using biased, unscientific methods. The public is then misled, and this can have an impact on election outcomes or the passing of public policy.

Push polls may be even more problematic. As stated, push polls are not really polls; yet the respondent is led to believe that the interviewer is conducting legitimate research. Push polls have two negative effects. First, respondents can become skeptical of polls and refuse to participate in legitimate polling. Pollsters are having increasing difficulty getting willing participants;[42] push polling only accentuates the problem.

Second, and perhaps more important for the purposes of a healthy democracy, push polls contribute to the public's cynicism toward government. The negative information provided by push pollsters only adds to many people's beliefs that politics is dirty, politicians are corrupt, and the electoral process is flawed. Some scholars argue that the entire purpose of push polling is to suppress voter turnout.[43] "It's unfortunate that this term 'push poll' ever achieved currency, because it's not a poll," said former AAPOR president Michael Traugott. "It makes people more cynical about politics, and that's something that democracy can't afford."[44]

Notes

1. National Council on Public Polls, press release, 22 May 1995.

2. Proffit, "Progress in Campaign Reform."

3. McInturff, "Partner, Public Opinion Strategies."

4. *Los Angeles Times* poll #466.

5. The results showed that more than half of the voters said they were not affected by this ad, 13% were more likely to vote for Riordan for governor, and 25% said they were less likely to do so.

6. Not everyone believes that persuasion calling or even balanced-negative poll questions are good for the political process. "The trouble is that even balanced surveys yielding unbiased responses will disseminate negative information," wrote Sabato and Simpson (*Dirty Little Secrets*, 247). "This adversely affects the tenor and character of the campaign, and adds to the rampant negativism of modern politics."

7. National Council on Public Polls, press release.

8. Sabato and Simpson, *Dirty Little Secrets*, p. 244.

9. Traugott and Kang, "Push Polls as Negative Persuasive Strategies."

10. Sabato and Simpson, *Dirty Little Secrets*.

11. Bumiller, "Giuliani Accuses Mrs. Clinton of Negative Calls," p. B6.

12. Nagourney and Murphy, "Attack on Cole Is Raised," p. A1.

13. Cardwell, "Badillo Accuses Bloomberg of Conducting Smear Campaign."

14. Ibid.

15. Ibid.

16. Lynch had defaulted on student loans and had been arrested three times during the 1970s and 1980s.

17. Guarino, "'Push Poll Firm IDs Client."

18. Guarino, "'Push Pollsters in 9th Implicated Elsewhere."

19. Connolly and Manning, "What 'Push Polling' Is," p. A21.

20. Yardley, "Calls to Voters," p. A1.

21. The preceding questions were listed in the *New York Times* on 14 February 2000 in a section titled "At a Glance—Pointed Questions" on p. A16.

22. Rich, "Everybody into the Political Mudfight," p. A15.

23. Ironically, John McCain hired Public Opinion Strategies to do polling during the 2000 primaries. Public Opinion Strategies had been tied to conducting push polls in the past (Van Natta, "Years Ago"). Even more ironic, Bill McInturff, whose letter we cited earlier blasting the use of push polls, is a partner with Public Opinion Strategies.

24. Dawson, "Day Accused of Playing Dirty Poll," p. 3.

25. "Labor Accused of Push Polling."

26. Traugott and Kang, "Push Polls as Negative Persuasive Strategies."

27. House of Representatives Home Page, "Push Poll Disclaimer Act."

28. Traugott and Kang, "Push Polls as Negative Persuasive Strategies," p. 295.

29. Fox, "Push Polling," p. 593.

30. Ibid., p. 592.

31. Ibid.

32. Bull, "Bill Would Prohibit," p. C-10. How one determines whether a poll violates the proposed law is unclear.

33. Ibid.

34. Fox, "Push Polling," p. 589.

35. Ibid., p. 584.

36. Asher, *Polling and the Public*, 5th ed., p. 137. Citizens should be skeptical of any instant poll, regardless of whether it is a dial-in poll, because pollsters do not have the opportunity to call back missed respondents.

37. Traugott, "Assessing Poll Performance," p. 404.

38. Ibid., p. 405

39. Morris, *Vote.com*, p. 118.

40. Ibid., p. 120.

41. Ibid.

42. Asher, *Polling and the Public*, 5th ed.

43. Sabato and Simpson, *Dirty Little Secrets*.

44. Daves, "Push Polling Controversy," p. 28A.

7

Are Exit Polls Bad for Democracy?

Gerald C. Wright

Editors' note: Since this writing, exit polls have undergone more scrutiny and criticism. In the 2002 midterm elections, after an overhauling of the Voter News Service (VNS), computer malfunctions kept news outlets from obtaining exit poll data. Shortly afterward, the major news organizations dismantled VNS. However, the networks have indicated that they remain committed to exit polling. The problems of 2002 and the dismantling of VNS in no way change Wright's support of exit polling as crucial to studying voting behavior and election outcomes.

Exit Polls as Public Enemy

The media and politics merge on the nights of U.S. presidential elections to provide one of the most riveting spectacles of our national politics. It provides the grandeur of a free people selecting their leaders in a democratic celebration of the peaceful transfer of power and combines this with suspense—at least in some years—of a national "who dunit," only in this case it is "who's gonna' get it?" The "it" of course is the presidency, easily the most visible, followed, and powerful position in the world. Election night, thus understandably captures

I would like to thank Jeanette Morehouse for her assistance in compiling the materials used in this essay.

the attention not only of Americans, but also of observers across the globe. With so much at stake, and with huge audiences, the broadcast media, especially television, gear up to do their level best at reporting on the election in ways that will bring prestige to their networks and viewers for their sponsors.

Out of this volatile mix of media and politics has grown the highly controversial offshoot of scientific polling called the "exit poll," which collects information gathered from large samples of citizens as they leave their polling places. Exit polls ask, first and foremost, who the voters have cast their ballots for, and also some information about the voters themselves to enable analysts to get at class, race, and religious cleavages that may be at work in the election. They typically also include a few questions about perceptions of the candidates' qualities and the voter's positions on some of the issues that were prominent in the campaign. To meet their needs the media invented these exit polls, which have now become fixtures of national, and many state, elections.

The exit polls represent quite a substantial investment by the media. In 2000, the Voter News Service, which is the major exit poll organization and about which I will say more below, had a budget of $35 million. With this budget, they harvest information that is to serve the two principal goals of election night coverage: to tell us who is winning and to explain the voters' decisions. For this investment, one would think that smart businesspeople like those running the network news organizations would see a favorable return in terms of a higher level of precision and depth of explanations of election night reporting. Instead, for many postelection commentators, the chief result of exit polling has been to debase democracy and to show the recklessness of media in their pursuit of ratings.

Consider some of the language used to describe the media's contribution to Election Night 2000. Headlines proclaimed "the big mistake" and the *Columbia Journalism Review* condemned "hair trigger projections,"[1] while the *Christian Science Monitor* reported on what it called "egregious mistakes" and said "the biggest problem on election night was the media's use of exit polling."[2]

On the other side of the world, election night was headlined as "Technology Goes Mad in Polling,"[3] and the thesis was offered that the American media's use of technology would increase America's cynicism. Allan Lichtman argued that the media are "turning the presidential elections into something like horse racing, driven solely by the poll." Lichtman wrote that the media had "to get rid of these pernicious polls" and suggested that the networks were attempting to whip up "artificial drama."[4] Another saw it as a night in which TV's talking heads were "humbled and humiliated."[5] The British description of Election Night 2000 is the most interesting: "a debacle of million dollar gadgetry and pseudo-science" in which an anxiously awaiting world "has been force fed ersatz omniscience."[6] Still more colorful was the description of election night projections as "premature statistical ejaculations."[7] In the United States, it was described as "the greatest train wreck in modern US media history,"[8] a "media meltdown" with a list of TV networks, Web sites, and newspapers making up a "dishonor roll."[9] The *Toronto Sun* simply told its readers that "the exit polls were wrong, wrong, wrong."[10]

Following the election, three high-level study commissions were formed to look at what happened in 2000 and to decide what changes should be made. The National Commission on Federal Election Reform, headed by former presidents Ford and Carter, made a host of recommendations, including an embargo on any election projections based on exit polls until polls had closed across the country (except Hawaii and Alaska). CNN instituted its own blue-ribbon study of Election Night 2000, and it too found much fault with how exit polls were analyzed and reported.[11]

What happened that focused so much ridicule on the networks and caused them such intense self-scrutiny? Two mistakes, both dealing with the outcome of the presidential election in the state of Florida, were made. Simply put, the media stumbled badly in calling the presidential outcome in Florida. All five networks (ABC, CBS, NBC, CNN, and Fox News) first said that Al Gore was going to carry Florida. Given how the election seemed to be going in other states when the announcement was made, it appeared that if Gore were to win Florida he very likely would be the next president. However, the call for Gore was premature and was retracted. Later, the media reported that George W. Bush was the winner in Florida. Then, in the wee hours of the morning, they had to retract the call for Bush as well, and the 2000 election was launched into a confusing new world of counts and recounts with lawyers and courts stepping in to decide who had actually won in Florida.

Election 2000 was different from other elections in many respects, but 2000 was not the first time election night coverage and exit polling have been figuratively tarred and feathered by the print media—and it will probably not be the last time either. Where there is controversy and lots of media coverage, one can expect to find some legislators proposing laws to fix whatever bothers the critics, or at a minimum, to investigate. Following Election 2000, we were treated to hearings led by Representative W. J. (Billy) Tauzin (R-LA.), who, as chairman of the Committee on Trade and Communications, set out to examine the networks' errors, air his concerns about possible partisan bias in the projection models used by the networks, and generally drag the network heads over the coals for the mistakes made in 2000.

As the result of Tauzin's investigation, we were treated with a number of recommendations to avoid the problems of Election Night 2000 again. After looking more closely at the exit polls, their strengths and weaknesses, and how they are conducted and interpreted, we will be in a good position to evaluate some of the recommendations that have been made. These suggestions are important to analyze, because elections are vital to the health of democracy and anything that affects the fair and open functioning of the electoral process may constitute an obstacle to democracy. To let the reader know where we are headed, I will argue that the networks' coverage of the presidential election generally, and the use of exit polls in particular, poses no threat to American democracy and that government regulation is not needed. The critics have not stopped to carefully examine the likely effects of their recommendations or the implications of implementing them on the operation of free elections.

What Are Exit Polls and Why Do We Have Them?

To evaluate the contribution—or damage—exit polls do, we need to understand the context that gave rise to them. That is, why do the media conduct these polls at all? Most national polls are for many purposes interchangeable in the sense that once one has a random sample of respondents, she can ask about room deodorizer or vacation preferences as well as about politics. In fact, quite a few polling firms make their money doing market research using essentially the same methods and technology during the "off-season." Exit polls, in contrast, are purely political, electoral, and media driven. They exist because the media compete with one another in providing coverage of the elections.

The challenge the networks face in covering elections is how to get viewers to watch their channels. Besides offering pleasing anchor personalities and the best graphics one can muster, a key audience draw is the ability to say something new and substantive about the election itself. For the election, an important goal is to be the first to announce the winner. While they consistently deny ever taking risks in "calling" a race, the networks are fully aware that more attention, and perhaps prestige—maybe even more viewers—goes to the network that is first. This necessarily means getting information about the outcome to viewers well before candidates decide to concede and way before election officials certify the winner.

In the 1960s in Kentucky, CBS News conducted the first exit poll, and they continued to develop the methodology of exit polling to provide election night filler and explanations.[12] It was not until the 1980s that the use of exit polls grew rapidly. All the major networks were running exit polls in most or all of the states in presidential election years, and they came to be relied upon more for making projections. Exit polls fill an important role because they provide information not available from other sources. Preelection polls are, by definition, completed before the election, which opens the way for two frequently damaging sources of error if they were to be relied upon on election night. One is determining who is going to vote. Because voting is a socially desirable behavior, respondents in preelection surveys frequently report that they will vote when in reality they do not. For example, it is not infrequent for 70% of respondents in a preelection poll during a presidential election year to confidently state they will vote, when in fact roughly half actually do. Since voters and nonvoters may differ in their preferences, it is risky to use preferences in preelection polls to predict who will win. Because of this problem, pollsters have attempted a variety of different question formats to filter out nonvoters, but so far they have had limited success.

The second problem that undermines the utility of preelection polls on election night is that vote intentions change. Preelection polls, if shut down too early, can miss last minute shifts that influence the election's outcome. That happened in 1980 when most of the preelection expectations were based on polls that had been completed the Thursday and Friday before the election. These polls indicated that the Carter/Reagan contest was going to be very close. However, the outcome was a landslide victory for Reagan. The change was actually caught early by Pat Caddell, Carter's pollster. He continued polling over the weekend and saw a clear shift in opinion as last-minute deciders almost uniformly went to Reagan. The way around getting caught by the combination of inflated promises to vote and last-minute swings in opinion is to catch people who vote, and right at the time they vote. Exit polls are uniquely suited for this task.

A possible alternative to using exit polls is for the networks to rely only on actual election returns as they come in and to infer from these results who voted how and why, as well (of course) as who won. However, there is a huge danger of misinforming the public when commentators rely solely on election returns to tell the election story.

The problem of what statisticians call "ecological fallacy" exists. If counties with more white-collar workers happen to vote for candidate X, and counties with more blue-collar workers vote for candidate Y, an observer may conclude that "the white-collar vote is going for candidate X." The truth is that there could be almost any kind of a mix of white-collar and blue-collar voters supporting the pair of candidates; indeed, the voters' choices may have nothing to do with worker status, but with other things correlated with it, like race, religion, or how the local economy is doing. In short, while actual returns are accurate in terms of votes cast, they do not tell us who voted for whom, and they certainly do not tell us why. Taking away valuable tools like the exit polls would, in effect, force election night analysts to wing it with bare election returns, and in the process they would almost inevitably get it wrong as often as they got it right.

Exit polls provide a solution to the problems we have just discussed. We know the people in the sample actually voted, because the interviewer catches them coming out of the voting booth. Second, the interview is as close to the actual vote as possible, so there is no possibility for opinion change (though the respondent could be lying). Third, the exit polls provide a wealth of data to describe voting patterns by race, gender, and income, as well as by voters' policy positions and how they feel about the different candidates.

The use of exit polls in describing and interpreting election campaigns has really taken hold. Figure 7.1 shows the growth in stories using exit poll results in the *New York Times* and the *Los Angeles Times* from 1980 to 2001. The overall message is one of a clear increase with peaks in election years, especially presidential years and a drop-off in off years. If we look at the nations' top fifty newspapers, as determined by Lexis-Nexis, we can see a similar dynamic, but one based on a much larger sample of newspapers (see figure 7.2).[13] It is interesting that only a small fraction of the media reports that use exit poll data are explaining or describing the election for which the data were gathered. The vast majority of these stories use the data to illustrate how voters made decisions in a past election as a means of discussing current election strategy, issues, and challenges to the candidates and parties.

In the 1980s, the three television networks (ABC, CBS, and NBC) were each running their individual exit polls. This is the period when exit polls came into their own as a source for projections of which presidential candidate would carry a state, as well as for projections of winners in contests for Congress and governor. For example, in 1982 CBS News and the *New York Times* conducted exit polls in most

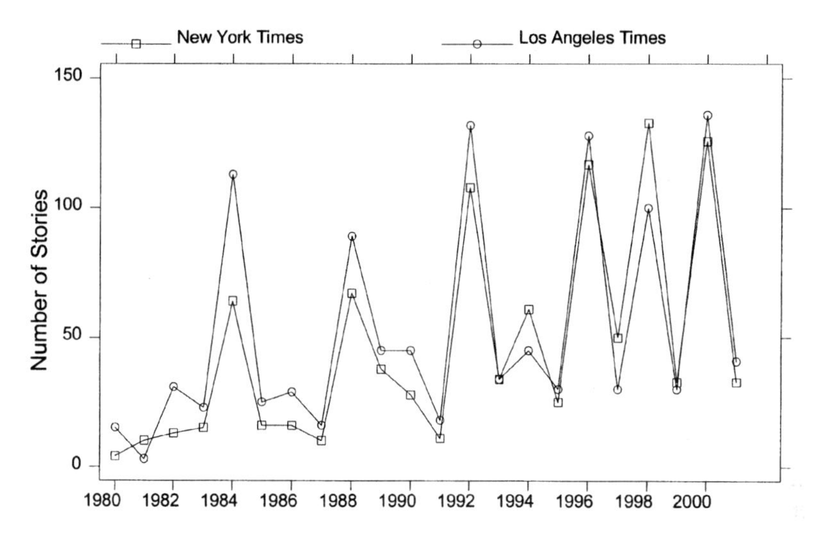

Figure 7.1. *New York Times* and *Los Angeles Times* Stories Using Exit Poll Data.

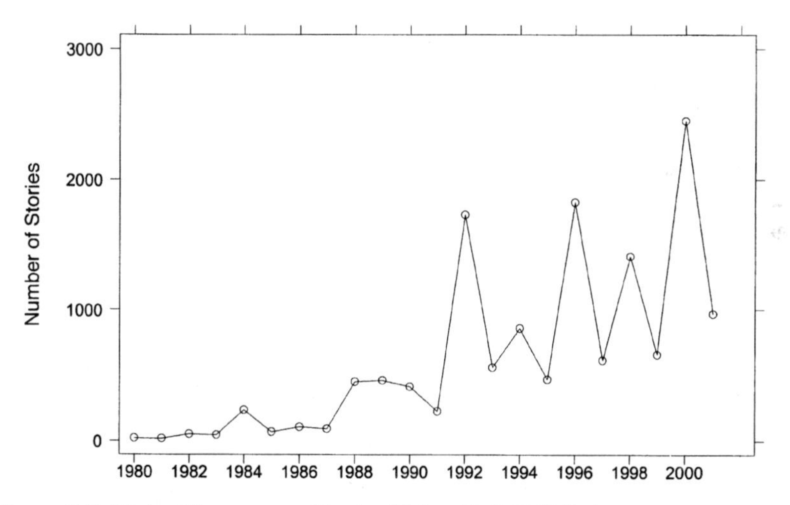

Figure 7.2. Major Newspaper Stories Using Exit Poll Data.

of the states in which there was a contest for U.S. senator, while in 1988 ABC News conducted exit polls in all fifty states. Much of the impetus for this increase in use was the successful reliance of NBC News on exit polls in the 1980 contest, which, as I mentioned, was thought to be close, but in fact was "called" early in the evening. For many of us who expected a long, enjoyable evening of electoral suspense, it was over before it started, and many blamed NBC for taking the suspense out of the evening.

Having the three networks each field their own exit polling operations was expensive, and so with pressures on newsrooms to cut costs, they agreed to jointly share the expense of conducting a set of exit polls. There was already a basis for a joint exit polling operation. Since the 1970s the media organizations had been sharing actual election returns through a jointly sponsored and supported organization called the News Election Service (NES). NES put into the field an operation with a person in virtually every county in the country making calls into a central office from the county clerks' offices with the actual returns as they came in from the precincts. In 1990, the networks took the next step in collective efforts with the formation of Voter Research and Surveys (VRS) to conduct exit polls. Warren Mitofsky, the longtime head of the survey unit at CBS News, ran VRS. In 1993, this organization morphed to form a new company, Voter News Service (VNS), which merged the functions of NES and VRS. ABC, CBS, NBC, CNN, Fox, and the Associated Press all sponsored the organization. VNS provided raw exit poll and vote returns data to the networks and AP, along with their own "vote projections" for the networks. At this juncture everyone was getting the same information from VNS, so, in theory, there would not be a great deal of competitive pressure to call races.

The theory was wrong; the pressure to be first with the news is an inherent part of journalism in America. In 1994, ABC News established its own "decision desk," complete with experts and computer models for projecting results, an operation apparently unknown to the other networks until election night. ABC "won" in making calls in several notable races that evening well ahead of the other networks, which relied only on VNS for making projections. ABC's competitors had no choice but to respond in kind with their own sets of experts and computer models. The competition for calls was as great as ever, but, unlike the 1980s, the networks were now all working off a common pool of exit poll returns. This did not cause many problems in the 1996 election, since Bill Clinton was expected to beat Bob Dole by a huge margin, and he did.

The arrangement in 2000 continued the 1996 format. Voter News Service had its headquarters in New Jersey and its computer operation in the World Trade Center. These were hooked to exit poll interviewers across the country, and VNS took that information and fed the decision desks of the sponsoring partners. I will discuss what happened on Election Night 2000, but first it will be informative to look briefly at the history of accuracy of VNS and why exit polls can go wrong.

How Accurate Are the Exit Polls?

When assessing an enterprise like VNS, it is important to lay out the basis for an evaluation. Part of that means being clear about the objectives of the enterprise. VNS supplies exit poll and vote return information to its media sponsors, and the purpose of this information is to provide bases for projections of the winners and for explanation of the vote trends and outcomes. The first is easy to assess; we know if the media project the wrong winner, and because it is so clear when they are wrong, that is where most attention about the quality of network evening coverage has centered. Explanations that commentators offer are much harder to verify because, by their very nature, they are more complicated than "Gore won" or "Bush won." Indeed, political science elections specialists typically work for years, using highly sophisticated statistical models, to try to determine which factors actually accounted for the voters' decisions. More often than not their analyses reflect a complex reality and have more factors interacting in convoluted ways than any election night anchor—or audience—would want to deal with. Political scientists have traditionally relied on the longer, more in-depth postelection surveys conducted by the National Election Studies (NES) at the University of Michigan for their data. These interviews ask hundreds of questions and can last over an hour, which is quite different than exit poll interviews that last a few minutes and usually have only about thirty questions.[14]

Over time the networks' projections have been amazingly accurate. By VNS's account, they have gotten over 99.8% of the races they projected correct.[15] That is impressive, but perhaps not quite as impressive as it initially sounds. It usually takes no information at all to be right 50% of the time; just flip a coin. Moreover, even casual political observers can probably get between 80% and 90% of the contests correct. Some contests are not contests at all: congressional incumbents win well over 90% of their reelection bids. In addition, some places are safe for one party. So, 99.8% is good—certainly better than most individuals could do—but the baseline for informed judgment against which this figure should be evaluated is probably something like 95%, not zero and not 50%.

Being right has an interesting downside for the networks; there is such a thing as being too good at predicting elections. Above I mentioned that the preelection polls suggested that the 1980 presidential election between the Democratic incumbent Jimmy Carter and the Republican challenger Ronald Reagan would be close. Exit polls that year showed a surprisingly strong Reagan trend. By 6:30 P.M. EST the networks were hinting at a big Reagan victory, and at 8:15 P.M. EST NBC declared Reagan the winner. At this point, a third of the central time zone polls and all of the western states' polls were still open. Rather than being admired for their successful exploitation of this new technology, the networks were chastised. They were said to be disenfranchising voters and causing alienation among those whose votes were now seen as meaningless.[16]

The 1980 "success" caused a lot of anguish among pollsters, academics, and media people. In fact, all sorts of dire things were hypothesized to follow from citizens hearing that the election was really over before it was over. Some argued that people would just not bother to vote. Others thought that people would change their votes and jump on the bandwagon or, conversely, feel sorry for the loser and there would be an underdog effect. Another possible hypothesis of the early returns was that knowing the winner would encourage citizens "to send them a message" by voting for protest candidates, safe with the knowledge that one would not have to live with the consequences of a message candidate in the White House.

Reacting to this backlash, almost all of it without a shred of evidence for the effects critics claimed, the networks promised not to call the election until all the polls had closed.[17] In addition, they promised not to call a state until "the great majority" of precincts were reported. The networks' reactions as a result of 1980 suggest a couple of problems, and these continued through the 2000 election. The first problem is that we really do not know much about the effects of projections on voter behavior. Earlier research suggested hardly any noticeable effects, which is not really surprising. The cases for bandwagon and underdog effects are equally uncompelling. Political scientists' theories of voter behavior do not offer any clear expectation of what to expect. On the other hand, more recent reports suggest that there is likely to be a small decrease in turnout among certain types of voters.[18] The second problem with the networks' reactions is that not announcing the winner of the election, when they already have this information, is in effect suppressing information. This is highly elitist behavior. The networks are implicitly saying to the electorate, "We know who is going to win, but for your own good, we are not going to tell you." Withholding information in a free and open election can be seen as an ironic—maybe even dangerous—behavior for the very organizations whose job it is to inform the public. We will return to consider these problems at the conclusion when we evaluate some of the proposals for reform that have been suggested.

There is usually no controversy when the networks' anchors "call" a state for a presidential candidate, or they put a congressional or gubernatorial seat into the Republican or Democratic column, because the vast majority of the projections are right. But the mistakes stand out. Even so, VNS had only one miscall in the 1990s: the New Hampshire Senate election in 1996. The networks called the race for the Democrat, but, after the votes were counted the Republican Bob Smith was declared the winner. However, VNS's claim is based on just one way of counting what constitutes "errors."

The network "calls" can have an impact even if they do not make a mistake in naming the winner. One example comes from a network variant of the exit polls called the "entrance polls" used in the Louisiana Republican caucuses in 1996.[19] On-air reports based on these polls exaggerated Pat Buchanan's victory over Phil Gramm.[20] Similarly, the networks and AP relied on exit polls in the Arizona primary to declare that Bob Dole was going to finish third behind Steve Forbes and Pat Buchanan when, in fact, he finished second.[21] The fear is that such projections, while technically not miscalling the winner of a contest, color perceptions of candidate strength and thereby affect their momentum.

Network reporting can also affect how people see the outcome of a race. In the 1989 gubernatorial race, Douglas Wilder became the first black governor in the United States, and as such the contest received considerable national attention. Wilder's actual margin of victory was less than 1%, but he was announced to be winning by 10%, a far bigger margin of victory. As a result, many viewers may have had the impression that Wilder won handily, when, in fact, he squeaked into office. The apparent cause of this overreport was a "social desirability" effect, in which some percentage of whites reported voting for Wilder when they really voted for his opponent, presumably because of race.[22] A similar pattern occurred in the New York City mayoral race held on the same day; the preelection and exit polls showed a significantly inflated margin of support for the black Democratic candidate, David Dinkins, in his narrow victory over Rudolph Giuliani.[24]

The point here is that in the overwhelming number of instances, the networks get it right. They provide useful information about the election and about what voters are thinking, and they are able to say who is winning well before the official results are announced. There remain a small number of cases where networks have clearly made mistakes. With network prestige on the line, and such a huge investment in calling the races correctly, how can the errors happen?

How Election Night Predictions Go Bad

We are familiar with what happened to get critics so excited on Election Night 2000. The networks first called the crucial state of Florida for Gore, then they took it back. Hours later they said Bush was the winner (which at the hour meant he had also won the presidency); and then they had to take *that* back. When we look closely at the events that led to these errors, we find that virtually none of the critics of exit polls and network coverage that I quoted toward the beginning of this chapter had it right. In their fervent calls for journalistic accuracy, they did not bother to find out how the process works in general and what happened in Florida on election night specifically. To understand what happened, we need to understand the basics of polling and how they apply to exit polls.

All modern polling rests on the obscure mathematics of probability theory, which allows pollsters to say how certain they are of their results. Probability theory is behind the frequent statements one encounters in poll reports that, for example, the actual results are "95% certain to within a plus/minus 3.5%" of the reported percentage. This crucial element of the process rests on a set of assumptions that underlie probability theory and tells pollsters about the likely sizes of error in their samples. These assumptions, interestingly, are never fulfilled completely in real-world polls.For example, probability theory assumes that one has a complete list of the population one wants to generalize, which is rarely the case. The challenges for exit polls begin with the fact that there is no list of voters (the population). There are lists of registered voters held by the county clerks and local elections officials across the country, but these are of varying quality and accuracy, and one does not know who will actually vote in any case. In addition, not everyone cooperates and, as we saw above, not everyone tells the complete truth.

The projections the networks make rest on three kinds of data: exit polls, sample precincts, and past voting returns that serve as a benchmark by which to measure the current election. Let us look briefly at each.

With exit polls, the strategy is to get a representative sample of voters in the states. As I just noted, the problem is that there are no reliable lists of those who will actually vote in the election. The networks therefore take samples of precincts. However, precincts do not vote, voters do, and turnout is higher in some precincts than others. The exit polls attempt to adjust for this fact by initially setting the number of interviews to be taken as proportional to past turnout in the precincts. The difficulty here is that relative turnout rates change with the differing attractiveness of candidates; the intensity of the campaigns waged in different locales; and the effectiveness of the parties, interest groups, and candidates at voter mobilization. The polls attempt to compensate for these factors by tracking turnout through the day and weighting results to reflect any expected changes in turnout. This is at best an inexact process, although it is certainly better than ignoring changes in relative turnout.

Another difficulty is the problem of interviewer discretion and confusion. It would seem to be pretty straightforward to produce a clean set of instructions that tells the interviewers to take every, say, fourth person as he or she comes out of the voting place. In reality, it is anything but straightforward. Consider, for example, the immense challenge of training and supervising the 45,000 people hired to report and process data for VNS. Anecdotal evidence hints at the problems and challenges. There are stories of interviewers who feared being late for work, so they interviewed everyone early to be sure to get their quota; or consider the poor interviewer who had to stand outside of a building that served more than one precinct. How could she possibly know which precinct the voters lived in? There is also some documentation that VNS workers interview people who appear willing to be interviewed.

Yet another problem interviewers face is refusal rates. In some places almost half of those asked refuse to participate in the surveys. In addition, we know that those who refuse are not the same as those who willingly cooperate. Interviewers are asked to note the gender, race, and estimated age of those who refuse, and the exit poll experts use this information to develop weights that, they hope, correct distortions induced by refusals. This helps, to be sure, but it is not a guarantee. The 1992 New Hampshire Republican presidential primary provides an illustration. The networks predicted Buchanan to do better than he actually did. Postelection analysis suggested the cause: his supporters were more adamant, and they wanted their protest choice to be heard. President Bush's (the elder) supporters were less enthusiastic and were more likely to refuse to participate in the exit poll.

Election 2000 revealed a new source or error. The infamous butterfly ballot that confused many voters in Palm Beach County, Florida is only a specific instance of a general problem, and yet it constitutes a different challenge for the exit polls.[24] Ballot formats differ quite substantially across the country. Although we are unlikely to see much more of the butterfly ballot, there are still tremendous differences in the form and manner of voting. In some places, candidates' names appear on a touch screen, while in others their names are arranged in different orders and the vote is registered by pulling a lever or filling in dots on a sheet to be read electronically. Each of these forms can influence vote choice in subtle ways, sometimes causing voter confusion. In contrast, the exit poll ballots respondents are asked to fill out have a common format, tailored only to the names of candidates in the local context and sometimes a few state-specific questions. We do not know if differences in the format between the real ballot and the exit poll ballot introduce error, but the significant levels of voter confusion induced by ballot design in Florida suggest this is a distinct possibility.

On top of these kinds of error that creep in as a matter of practice are the errors that theory tells us will occur, even if everything is done correctly. When networks announce poll results and say there is a 95% chance the actual figure is within something like plus-or-minus 3.5%, there is also 5% chance that the real number is more then 3.5 percentage points from the poll result. If one extends that across all the estimates made in an election evening, we quickly realize some of the estimates are going to be wrong. The problem is that the networks cannot know which of the estimates are off until after they have publicly committed to their projections and the official results are in.

Most of the time the occasional oddball sample that produces a less accurate estimate does not cause a big problem. For example, if the sample estimate of a U.S. Senate election is off by 6%, it does not get too many people upset if the actual winning margin is 10 or 15%. It is where the sample estimate is in error in close races that the potential for public embarrassment exists. And that is exactly what happened in Florida.

What Happened in Florida?

There were actually two mistaken calls in Florida and each has a quite different explanation. On the initial announcement that Gore would win Florida, Warren Mitofsky, who was working the CBS/CNN decision desk that night and who has as much experience with exit polls as anyone, explained that, combining all three sources of information used for projections, the early call for Gore was entirely justified. The exit polls suggested Gore would win by 5 to 10%, and estimates based on the sample precincts were that Gore's margin would be even larger. With this confluence of evidence, the CBS/CNN desk was quite confident in making the projection for Gore. Interestingly, Mitofsky pointed out that if the call had depended only on exit poll data, they would have not have made it. Those data, by themselves, were not strong enough.[25]

Where did the Gore call go wrong? It appears to have been in the selection of sample precincts and the election baseline used for comparison. The art in selection of sample precincts is to choose those that one believes will closely mirror what other precincts in the state will do in the current contest. Just by chance, one can get a sample of precincts that will go more for Bush or more for Gore than will the state at large. An additional piece of information used is how the behavior of the sample precincts compares with their behavior in earlier elections. If the current election is more Democratic or more Republican than in the baseline election, it can alert analysts to how the state will vote. However, this is useful only if the current results very closely track the relative strengths of the parties in the baseline election. In 2000, the precincts were selected and compared to the 1998 gubernatorial contest. That contest saw Jeb Bush get elected governor, so it seemed logical that, with another Bush on the ballot, the 2000 presidential election would closely align with the 1998 results. Although the VNS and network analysts deal with precincts, we can illustrate the nature of the problem using Florida's counties. Figure 7.3 shows the scatterplot of the 2000 presidential election with the county outcomes for the 1998 gubernatorial contest. It is apparent that vote for president and vote for governor are highly related; counties that went strongly for Jeb Bush also went strongly for George W. Bush. But this is not a perfect relationship, and the underlying assumption of using sample precincts and comparing current results to those of a past election is that the counties would all align on a straight line. To the extent that they depart from a straight line, the comparison between the current and baseline elections becomes less useful for prediction purposes. Consider, for example, the spread among the counties where Jeb Bush got just over 60% of the vote. If, by chance, precincts voting like the county indicated by the "A" were selected into the sample, then when the vote for president in 2000 came in at 50% it would suggest that George W. Bush was losing badly, running fully 10% behind what his brother did. However, if more precincts were selected that voted like county B, one would tend toward concluding that "W" was going to do even better than his brother, and hence win handily. Before the election, the analyst does not know which of these precincts (or

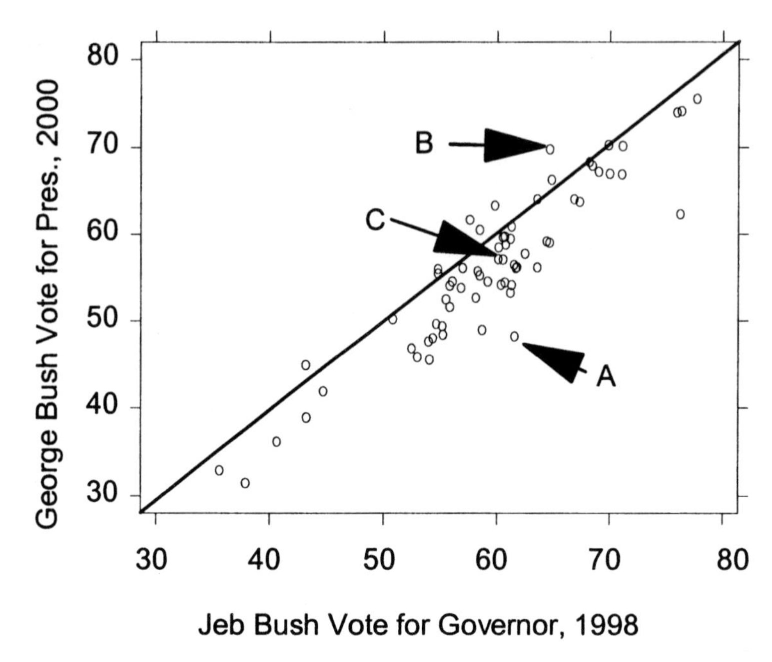

Figure 7.3. Comparison of 1998 Voting in Florida Counties with 2000.

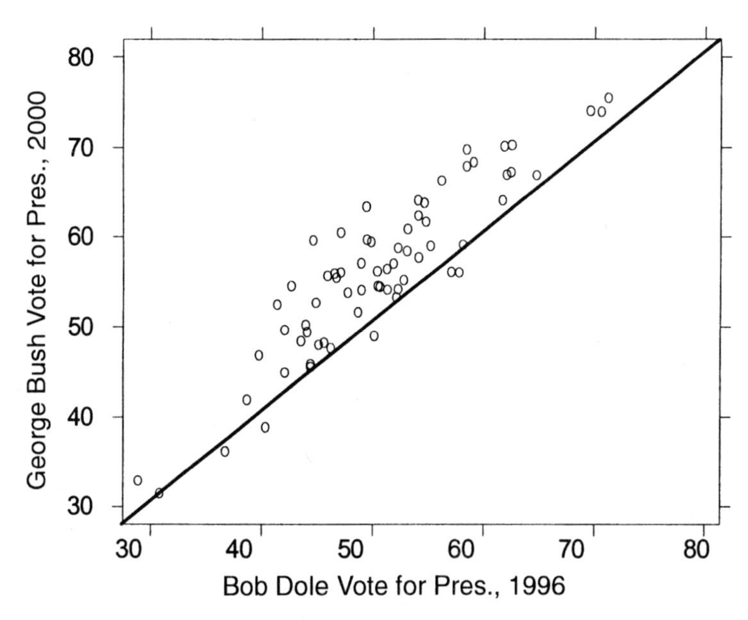

Figure 7.4. Comparison of 1996 Voting in Florida Counties with 2000.

in our hypothetical example counties) are in the sample. If one gets, by bad luck, a sample of precincts that are like B or A, rather than like C (which is more representative), the pattern of results in the sample precincts are not going to accurately reflect what is happening statewide.

Besides getting an unrepresentative sample by chance, there is an additional risk that the analyst will select an incorrect baseline race. In fact, one of the election postmortems suggested that the 1996 presidential race would have been a more appropriate base than the 1998 gubernatorial race. After the fact we can examine this "what-if." Figure 7.4 shows the 2000 vote for Bush in Florida's counties in a scatterplot with the 1996 vote for Bob Dole. At the extremes the match is quite nice, but in the middle range, there are a troubling number of departures as the scatter gets pretty wide. This suggests that had the analysts used the 1996 contest, they might have been in even worse shape in calling the election.

In relying on sample precincts compared to a past election, the analyst is banking on history largely repeating itself—that one contest will be basically a replay of an earlier contest, with the outcome shifting a reasonably uniform amount everywhere. However, losing candidates will not want the outcome to remain the same. The losing side would be stupid to say "let's do what we did last time and make similar appeals to the same voters and hope we are more convincing this time." Instead, they will try to construct a slightly amended coalition, stressing some issues that were not important before, downplaying some others, and even switching positions on others. The choices are not the same, and the campaigns are different. As a result, different constituencies will respond in various ways rather than moving all in the same direction an equal amount. This criticism is a fair one in that it is true that the last thing parties want to do is repeat a previous election they lost. But in defense of the projection analysts, many elections do look very much like earlier contests. The trick is determining which of the past elections is most like the current one, and that is where the risk comes in.

The rapid growth in many jurisdictions of absentee balloting is another problem that confronts exit pollsters. The analysts make assumptions about the level of absentee voting and how this will break down compared to the votes cast on Election Day. Typically, absentee voters are more Republican. The VNS models assumed for Florida in 2000 there would be a 7% absentee vote; in reality, absentee ballots comprised 12% of the electorate, which means the overall vote was going to come in more Republican than initial precinct-based estimates suggested.

In summary, on the first bad call, there are lots of sources of error, but given the technology available and the evidence at hand, the call for Gore was defensible. It was unfortunate for the networks that the bad call happened in connection with a state that was so close and so crucial to the outcome of the entire contest, but nevertheless, it was defensible.

The same cannot be said about the call for Bush. As the evening wore on, it became evident that the then-undecided Florida vote would determine the presidency. It was after 2:00 A.M. EST that the mounting results started looking promising for Bush. He had a 51,000 vote margin with 97% of the precincts reporting. The analysts calculated that Gore would need 63% of what were thought to be 179,000 outstanding votes. Getting that percentage was deemed highly unlikely. Only Palm Beach County offered the possibility of Gore gaining substantial votes, and it had 98% of its precincts already reported. At that point, based on counting real votes, Fox News decided to call the state for Bush, and everyone but AP and VNS fell into line in quick succession. After thirty minutes, the picture reportedly looked even better for Bush. But then it began to get blurry.

As the official votes came in and figures were rechecked, it became apparent that Bush's margin of victory would be uncomfortably small; it was certainly smaller than expected when the networks called Florida for Bush, and maybe there would be no Bush margin at all. Two errors were made, and both were avoidable.[26] The first was an error in estimating the number of votes not counted. Instead of 179,000 votes outstanding, there were actually 400,000 votes to be counted. This meant that Gore had much more room to make up votes and to overcome the Bush lead. The second was a VNS inputting error in Volusia County that made Bush look like he had twenty thousand votes more than he actually had. Both of these errors could have been caught with better communication and by checking incoming data against available information. As the consequence of these human errors, which worked their way through the system, the network decision teams began to recommend retracting the call made almost two hours earlier for Bush. So the networks put Florida back in the undecided column. Underlying these errors, according to the report CNN commissioned, was a breakdown in the communications between VNS and its client organizations. VNS knew about some errors in the database, and removed them without alerting the network decision teams. This action may have contributed to the readiness to miscall the election for Bush that evening. In addition, more careful checking of the data, including using information available from AP and from the Florida secretary of state's Web site, might have alerted the decision teams to the mistakes.

The consequences of the erroneoous calls are hard to estimate. The authors of the CNN report make it sound like a dark day for American politics. Those calls and their retractions constituted a "news disaster that damaged democracy and journalism."[27] If that is what happened, then that is very bad. I now take a closer look at what damage was really done and evaluate some of the recommendations that have been offered to improve the system.

Conclusions

It is not at all clear how democracy has been damaged. Many citizens contend that the wrong person became president, but regardless of how one feels about a president who did not carry the popular vote nationally, it is a stretch to connect bad calls and their retractions to the outcome of the 2000 election. The calls certainly led to some embarrassment, especially for the networks. At CBS, Dan Rather's summation shortly after the network called Florida for Bush will be remembered for his folksy and colorful overstatement: "Sip it, savor it, cup it, photostat it, underline it in red, press it in a book, put it in an album, hang it on a wall—George Bush is the next president of the United States." When things are put this strongly, rather than given the caution appropriate to estimates made on inherently fallible data, the commentators look silly when the results come out differently. Rather certainly acknowledged this fact when, after the network retracted its second call of the night, he told the audience, "If you're disgusted with us, frankly, I don't blame you." There were extended apologies and self-criticism in the weeks that followed, but an embarrassed media does not equal an abuse of democracy. Who else was hurt because of the Florida miscalls? It is arguable that Al Gore lost momentum. He was said, for a while, to have won Florida, but later Bush was said to have won not only Florida, but the presidency. Did this give Bush a perceptual advantage entering the chaos that became the Florida recount? It is very hard to argue that with any confidence. Analysis of the media's subsequent framing of the election seemed to be more affected by the decisions of the Florida secretary of state than by anything that was said in the network newsrooms on election night.[28]

To conclude, I would like to consider the critics' concerns and some of the recommendations that have been put forth. First, most of the critics' claims about the negative effects of calling an election (either early or mistakenly) are unsubstantiated. We know in detail what went wrong, but none of the critics we have encountered have been the least bit articulate about how democracy was abused. There have been claims since the 1960s that somehow if voters on the West Coast know how voters in the East cast their ballots, they will change their behavior. Studies over the years have not found any substantial evidence to back up these claims. As mentioned, whatever effects exist seem to be in the form of slight influences on turnout among specific types of voters. The conclusion of numerous studies is that, at best, the effects are very limited, and only a small subset of the population may have reacted to the announcements.

Recommendations

Let us consider some of the recommendations that have been made. This is not a full catalog, but it is a good sample.

DEMOCRATIC BIAS. In his hearings, Rep. Tauzin expressed concerns about an unintentional "Democratic bias" in the networks' exit polling and projections. His concern was that an inordinate number of contests that were predicted early in the evening were called for the Democrats. He argued that if the networks favored one party, the government might have to step in to make the coverage objective. Tauzin's concern is without foundation because the networks are in competition with one another. They want to be first in their predictions whether this helps Democrats or Republicans. The economics of competition insure that the networks will put forth the best and most accurate projections they can. In fact, the early calls were for Gore simply because the states where the returns were first available tended to be more Democratic.

CRIPPLE THE EXIT POLLS. Quite a number of politicians have attacked exit polls as the culprit. Some states have introduced and passed legislation requiring interviewers to stay some specified distance from the polling booths. Other politicians have urged voters to refrain from any interviewing until the polls have closed. Still others have admonished voters not to cooperate with exit polls, while in a number of states legislation is being considered that would actually prohibit any interviewing by exit pollsters until the voting booths are closed. Almost any government effort to regulate exit polls would be misguided. All of these measures to make it harder for the media to collect information from voters run afoul of the First Amendment. The measures would damage the quality of the exit polls and thereby produce a result in which citizens would know less about their election than is the case now. This is not a "benefit" for democracy that justifies pushing the limits of the First Amendment by telling networks how they should cover our elections.

UNIFORM CLOSING HOURS FOR VOTING. Some critics who worry about the effects of early announcements of trends, or even of the winner of the election, while polling booths are still open have suggested uniform closing hours nationwide. The objective of this recommendation is to keep the outcome from the electorate until everyone—or at least everyone living east of Alaska and Hawaii—has voted. Under the plan that some have put forward, the eastern time zone states would close their polls at 9:00 P.M. Daylight savings time would be shifted two weeks in the West so there would be only a two-hour difference between the coasts, thus allowing the voting in the West to conclude at 7:00 P.M. When all of the precincts were closed, the networks would be free to say who won.

This recommendation seems fine on the surface, but it is flawed as well. First, it would trample on the traditional division of labor that is central to our federal structure, and second, it would not work. The states run elections. We register to vote under the laws of our individual states; the officials and voting mechanisms are governed by state law. The federal government's only role is to insure that citizens' civil rights are not violated. To insist on uniform voting hours, however, takes away from the states one of their prerogatives. Some states try to maximize turnout by keeping their polls open later. This would penalize voters in western states who would have two fewer hours in the evening to exercise their right to vote than do voters in the eastern states. An unintended consequence might be lower turnout in the western states. It also builds in another inequity by forcing the eastern states to cover the costs of extended shifts for their election workers. It might make sense to sacrifice a state's traditional powers over elections and to impose some (presumably unfunded) mandates on a state if it would serve democracy in a clearly positive way. But it would not.

Second, uniform closing hours will not stop leaks about the course of the election based on information gleaned from the exit polls. The major networks are glad to promise to hold any discussion of exit polls until after the voting stops, but it is not a promise they are likely to keep. There are thousands of people involved in executing the exit polls. Every year early results are leaked, sometimes over the Internet and sometimes even on national news. In recent years *Slate, Salon,* or some other Internet source has leaked projections based on early exit polls for all to see. It is wishful thinking to believe that, when a local television or radio station reports these leaks and announces that X is going to win the election, the networks could or would sit on their data until polls closed. Voters will migrate to where the news is being reported, and the networks are not going lose audience share by voluntarily refusing to report. If the exit poll data exist, they will get out, because there is a tremendous market for it. It is that very market that gives rise to the collection of exit polls in the first place.

There is an even larger issue that applies to all of the recommendations and concerns about network election night reporting that I touched up on earlier in this chapter. The effort to control the exit polls interrupts the free flow of information in a democratic election. Who should have this right? As a nation, we have long said no one. The unfettered flow of information is a bedrock requirement for democratic elections. To say the networks can know an election outcome while the polls are open, but that the citizenry cannot be trusted with this information, reeks of elitism. This position is tantamount to some self-appointed information cops determining the bases of voters' decisions. The populist democratic view is that the only one who has a right to decide what information the voter should use in making his or her choices is the voter.

I have already argued that there has been no firm demonstration of a negative impact of announcing the state winner or even the election winner before everyone has voted. But, for the sake of argument, let us assume that the critics' fears are true that some people will change their votes and others will not vote at all if they learn whom the networks project to win the election. A supporter of democracy could still argue that people deciding not to vote because they know who is going to win is no reason to muzzle the press, and it is no reason not to air information that is obviously important enough for some voters that it actually affects their behavior.

The premise for the argument that the media should be free to broadcast whatever information their viewers want to hear is that voters have the right to make a decision on any basis they want. We allow them to vote for Gore because they like his stand on the environment or for Bush because of his stand on energy. We allow them to vote for Bush because they did not like Gore's behavior in the first debate, or even because they might be anti-Semitic and did not like Joe Lieberman, Gore's vice-presidential running mate. We allow voters to be influenced by television ads that do not tell the full truth and by candidate statements that are often distortions. In fact, we allow about half the population to not even vote, many for no good reason at all but that they do not want to bother. Although we can wish that voters were more informed and that candidates were more forthcoming with the truth, free elections mean voters can pick and choose the information they will use and the information they will ignore. This freedom logically implies that voters should also be able to act on the basis of who carried Pennsylvania or the entire East Coast, who Dan Rather thinks will carry Nevada, and who the analysts at the various networks project to win the entire election.

If a voter gets joy out of voting for who will win, she should know who is going to win. If the voter's major goal—that which will affect her behavior—is to be on the side of the underdog, that is her right as a free citizen. And if any voters really would leave a line where they are waiting to vote because the talking heads on television say "it's over" before the polls close, they should be able to do that, too. After all, they can leave because they are tired of waiting, or because they forgot to pick up something at the supermarket, or even because they want a Coke. Voters must be able to do what they want; allowing them to exercise this right does not damage democracy.

The federal government's role in elections should be minimal. There are tremendous temptations for those in power to alter the rules of the game in ways that are self-serving. Trying to structure what types of information the media can reveal about an election and what kind of information voters are allowed to have is not compatible with our democratic principles and, in the case of exit polls and election-night coverage, there is no reason to enter into this dangerous thicket.

This argument goes against most of what has been written about election-night coverage and the use of exit polls. How should we respond to the critics' concerns? And what should be done to make sure the media "gets it right" in the future? Leading figures in journalism like Joan Konner, James Risser, and Ben Wattenberg, who wrote the report chastising CNN for its coverage (albeit at CNN's request), stated that Election Night 2000 was a "news disaster that damaged democracy and journalism"[29] But just how was democracy damaged? It was not. Indeed, one could reasonably argue that democracy would survive quite well if the networks miscalled every election; that would only reveal that the networks are not good at predicting elections, and democracy has no requirements at all about Dan Rather's or Peter Jennings's or anyone else's ability to see into the future. For democracy, it just does not matter.

Was journalism set back? It was embarrassing, but it has to be entirely the network's decision whether they want at any point to take the risk of making announcements that could come back to haunt them later. Journalists are human, and close elections are, as we have discussed, quite hard to predict. It should be of no surprise to anyone that mistakes have been, and will be, made. The damage suffered by the media as a result of making a few honest mistakes pale by comparison to the disservice that would be done to the country and to the media themselves if they had to pick and choose what information about elections and candidates to release to the public. It seems the height of elitism to recommend that the media keep the secrets they find in the exit poll data to themselves when the public, for whatever reason, is interested. The next step would be to recommend that the media talk only about the "important" issues and not about "personalities." It is not uncommon to hear arguments that the media should stick with discussions of the environment, foreign affairs, the economy, and other serious issues. But this ignores and undercuts those voters who feel that the candidate's character, honesty, and leadership styles *are* the "important issues."

The flow of electoral information currently is regulated by a complex set of forces that includes the norms of journalism (with some outlets adhering more closely to these than others), the competitive need for audience share, and even the simple availability of information. These are entirely sufficient for journalism to be self-correcting. Indeed, we saw exactly that process at work following Election 2000. The networks looked closely at the errors that were made, and at the organization and funding of VNS, and they will make decisions about how to avoid such embarrassments in the future. They will probably continue to withhold projections "until the great majority" of precincts in a state have closed and reported the vote, but this action is more for public relations than of any real service to democracy. Indeed, there is no logical difference between a news program reporting that the preelection polls are indicating it will be a landslide victory for a candidate the day before the election and the same network saying the same thing on Election Day, but now basing that conclusion on what the networks judge to be even more reliable information.

Our conclusion, then takes us back to where we began. Election night is a wonderful celebration of a free people exercising their right to choose who will govern them. Election Night 2000 was no different. It was tremendously absorbing, it kept millions of people up much later than usual, and, in the end, it was fun. Millions learned that polls, even reasonably well-conducted exit polls and other prediction models, can be wrong, and that is not a bad thing for a public to know. The best recommendation—and no doubt the media will impose this on themselves for their own interest in avoiding embarrassment—is to be more candid about the level of uncertainty that is inherent in projections.[30] But even if they hedge their bets, the networks will either be wrong or later than someone else in stating who they think will win and why. And by the very nature of the process, some projections will be wrong, but that does not cause damage to democracy or to the quality of our elections. Exit polls are a source of solid information about who votes for whom and why. Without this information, the network anchors would just wing it anyway, relying on experts who guess at the very information the exit polls now produce. Exit polls are certainly not necessary for democratic elections, but they do provide useful, important, and highly interesting information. Regulating exit polling and changing election rules is a futile effort to quarantine the electorate from information about how their fellow citizens have voted and inconsistent with democratically free elections.

Notes

1. Hickley, "The Big Mistake."
2. "Exit Polls, Stage Left," p. 10.
3. *Australian,* 10 Nov 2000, p. 12.
4. Denwoodie, "Democracy the Loser in TV Poll Dramas," p. 15.
5. Collins, "Television a Picture of Shame," p. 22.
6. Preston, "Race for the White House," p. 2.
7. Gitlin, "Oops, I'll Say It Again," p. 13.
8. Lusetich, "Premature Evaluation," p. M01.
9. Collins, "Eye on the Media," p. A60.
10. Worthington, "Like Idiots, We Trusted the Box," p.16.

11. Information on the nongovernmental National Commission on Federal Election Reform can be found at <http://www.reformelections.org/index.php> while the CNN report on the 2000 election is available at <http://www.cnn.com/2001/ALLPOLITICS/stories/02/02/cnn.report/cnn.pdf.>.

12. Mitofsky, "Fool Me Twice," p. 36; Campbell and Palmquist, "Exit Polls as a Source of Political Data."

13. The use of exit polls has expanded well beyond our shores. In the last few years exit polls have played a large role in media reporting of national elections in countries including Brazil, Bulgaria, India, Ireland, Japan, the Philippines, Poland, Mexico, Romania, and Russia.

14. In recent years, political scientists have come to realize that each type of data collection may have advantages, depending on the kinds of questions that the researcher is pursuing. These are weighed by Campbell and Palmquist, "Exit Polls as a Source of Political Data."

15. "VNS Chief Reports on Exit Poll."

16. Tannenbaum and Kostrich, *Turned-On TV/Turned-Off Voters*, pp. 23–25.

17. Interestingly, these promises and concerns only apply to the continental forty-eight states. Apparently no one feels strongly enough about the contaminating effects of calling an election to wait the extra three hours for the polls to close in Alaska and Hawaii.

18. Meyer, "Stop Pulling Punches with Polls," summarizes the thin literature on this question.

19. Entrance polls, which involve getting voters' preferences as they enter the caucuses, save time, since the caucuses involve discussion and, therefore, delay in getting information back to the anchors.

20. Randolph, "Journalists Wield Polling Sword at Their Peril,."

21. Braxton, "TV's Early Call in Arizona Vote Angers Dole"; Campbell and Palmquist, "Exit Polls as a Source of Political Data."

22. Traugott and Price, "Exit Polls in the 1989 Virginia Gubernatorial Race."

23. Rosenthal, "Broad Disparities In Votes And Polls Raising Questions."

24. The Palm Beach County elections supervisor feared that the 2000 ballot, with its usual design of candidates in a list and check boxes next to the names would be too cramped, especially for her elderly voters with declining eyesight. In an effort to gain some space on the ballot she used a "butterfly ballot" that placed two columns with George W. Bush's name on the left and Pat Buchanan's on the right, and Gore's name below Bush's. The votes were to be registered by punching holes in the ballot, which were aligned in the middle. The ballot was confusing, and thousands of people who wished to vote for Gore actually voted for Buchanan. Without these errors, Al Gore in all likelihood would have received another 2,000 or so votes in Palm Beach County, and he would have won Florida and the election. See Brady et al., "Law and Data."

25. Mitofsky, "Fool Me Twice."

26. Ibid., pp. 37–38.

27. Konner, Risser, and Wattenberg, "Televisions Performance on Election Night 2000," p. 1.

28. Jamieson and Waldman, "The Morning After."

29. Konner, Risser, and Wattenberg, "Television's Performance on Election Night 2000," p. 1.

30. "CNN Announces Election Night Coverage Change Following 'Debacle'."

8

Deliberative Polling, Public Opinion, and Democratic Theory

James S. Fishkin

Democratic theory has struggled with how to combine two basic values—deliberation and political equality. Deliberation has long been thought to require a social context of small group, face-to-face communication, but political equality requires that everyone's views be counted equally. As a result, when political equality is applied to the large-scale nation-state, it has led to mass consultation of millions of persons, many of whom are barely paying attention. Hence there has long seemed to be a conflict between the aspiration for deliberation and the application of political equality.

The value of deliberation was clearly articulated by the Founding Fathers. They wanted institutions that would give expression not just to any public views, but also to those opinions that had been "filtered" so as to produce "the deliberative sense of the community." Representatives, the Founding Fathers believed, serve to "refine and enlarge the public views by passing them through a chosen body of citizens," as Madison argued in *Federalist* No. 10. "The public voice" pronounced by representatives under such a regulation "will be more consonant to the public good than if pronounced by the people themselves convened for the purpose."[1] Small deliberative bodies, such as the U.S. Senate or a constitutional convention, allow representatives to better determine the public good than just by bringing the people together and asking them. There is a difference, in other words, between the deliberative or thoughtful public opinion one can find in representative institutions, at least at their best, and the uninformed and unreflective preferences commonly found in the mass public.

The problem is how to reconcile this aspiration for thoughtful and informed preferences with political equality—with the aspiration for counting everyone's preferences equally. Deliberative bodies may represent highly informed and competent preferences, but only an elite often shares those preferences. Direct consultation of mass preferences will typically involve counting uninformed preferences, often simply reflecting the public's impressions of sound bites and headlines. Hence, the hard choice between politically equal but unreflective mass preferences and politically unequal but relatively more reflective elite views.

In other words, we seem to face a forced choice between elected and presumably well informed elites and uninformed masses. But there are institutional experiments with deliberation among representative microcosms of the mass public. These experiments, ranging from so-called citizens' juries to deliberative opinion polls, take random samples of the public and subject them to situations where they are effectively motivated to get good information, hear balanced accounts of competing arguments, and come to a considered judgment. These experiments show that ordinary citizens are capable of becoming informed and dealing with complex policy matters. And it is possible to get an input to policymaking that is representative of the mass public while, at the same time, embodying deliberation. There is also a sense in which, through random sampling, a notion of political equality is realized. Every citizen has (at least theoretically) an equal chance of being chosen through random sampling and an equal chance, once chosen, to have his or her preferences counted. Hence, random sampling embodies a form of political equality or equal consideration, just as would a system in which everyone participated.

This solution to the problem of combining political equality and deliberation was devised in ancient Athens, where deliberative microcosms of several hundred chosen by lot made many key decisions. However, this process was lost in the dust of history with the demise of Athenian democracy. When random sampling was revived for informal political consultation, it was employed, without deliberation, via public opinion polls. But the potential to combine random sampling with deliberation for the large-scale nation-state remained. The research program I will outline here, Deliberative Polling, is an attempt to build on this ancient insight.

It is worth noting that the initial launch of the public opinion poll actually combined scientific sampling with aspirations for deliberation. After the early triumph of the scientific public opinion poll, when Gallup correctly predicted the winner of the 1936 U.S. presidential election (while an inferior method, the self-selected *Literary Digest* poll, had predicted a landslide for Alf Landon over Franklin Roosevelt), Gallup reflected on the aims of the poll, which he then considered such a serious instrument of democratic reform that he called it the "sampling referendum." He argued that the combination of mass media and scientific sampling could bring the democracy of the New England town meeting to the large-scale nation-state. Gallup wrote

> Today, the New England town meeting idea has, in a sense, been restored. The wide distribution of daily newspapers reporting the views of statesmen on issues of the day, the almost universal ownership of radios which bring the whole nation within the hearing of any voice, and now the advent of the sampling referendum which produces a means of determining quickly the response of the public to debate on issues of the day, have in effect created a town meeting on a national scale.[2]

Gallup thought that he could use the poll to create on the large scale the deliberative democracy of the town meeting because the media would, in effect, put the whole country in one room, and the poll would allow for an assessment of the resulting informed opinion. He neglected to realize the effects of "rational ignorance"—the room was so big that no one was paying much attention. Instead of the democracy of the New England town meeting, he got the inattentive and often disengaged democracy of modern mass society. Instead of informed and deliberative public opinion, he got the kind of debilitated public opinion, based on a casual impression of sound bites and headlines, that is common in mass democracies throughout the world. Instead of reflective or "refined" opinion, he got only a reflection of "raw" opinion. Technology helped create a new form of democracy, but it was not one that realized the values of the town meeting. The town meeting, after all, offers the potential of combining deliberation with a consideration of everyone's views. But the trick, in democratic reform, is to pay enough attention to the social context that might really motivate thoughtful and informed public opinion and then to combine the realization of that social context with a process for selecting or counting the views of the participants equally.

The two basic questions that any form of democratic consultation must answer are: Who speaks for the people and what sorts of opinions do they represent? Deliberative Polling is based on a distinctive combination of answers to these two questions. As compared to self-selected forums or samples of convenience, it employs scientific random samples. And as compared to the snapshots of an inattentive public often offered by conventional polls, it assesses informed public opinion produced through deliberation. In this way, the Deliberative Poll attempts to represent everyone in a given population—through a statistical microcosm empowered to think about the issues in question under favorable conditions. Of course, a lot depends on what we mean by favorable conditions—a point to which I will return.

At its core, a Deliberative Poll is a survey of a random and representative sample of respondents, both before and after they have had a chance to deliberate. An ordinary poll offers a representation of public opinion as it is—even if that representation reflects no more than the public's impressions of sound bites and headlines on the issue in question. By contrast, a Deliberative Poll attempts to represent what the public *would* think about the issue if it were motivated to become more informed and to consider competing arguments.

But why go to all the trouble to conduct Deliberative Polls when a conventional poll can also solicit opinion from a good statistical microcosm, i.e., a scientific random sample? A great deal of public opinion research has established that the public is often not well informed about complex policy or political matters. Only a small percentage of the population can answer even the most basic questions. And other researchers have shown that policy-specific information can lead to dramatic changes of opinion under experimental conditions.[3]

The low information levels among the mass public should not be surprising. Anthony Downs coined the term "rational ignorance" to explain the incentives facing ordinary citizens.[4] If I have one vote in millions, why should I spend the time and effort to become well informed on complex issues of politics and policy? My individual vote, or my individual opinion, is unlikely to have any effect. And most of us have other pressing demands on our time, often in arenas where we can, individually, make more of a difference than we can in politics or policy. From the standpoint of democratic theory, this lack of effective incentives for individual citizens to become well informed is regrettable but also understandable.

In fact, many of the opinions reported in conventional polls may not even exist. They may be what Philip Converse termed "non-attitudes" or phantom opinions. Many respondents do not answer "don't know" (when they don't) and are more inclined to pick an alternative almost randomly.[5] And even those opinions that are not quite non-attitudes may be very much "off the top of the head" in that they reflect little thought or sustained attention.

Among methods of consultation, the Deliberative Poll is the most ambitious in aspiring to get informed opinion from a scientific random sample.[6] The Center for Deliberative Polling has conducted nineteen Deliberative Polls in various parts of the world since 1994. Nine of these have been national—five in Britain (on crime, Britain's future in Europe, the monarchy, the 1997 British general election, and the future of the National Health Service on its fiftieth anniversary in 1998), one in Denmark (on the euro right before the referendum in 2000), two in Australia (one before the republic referendum in 1999 and one on reconciliation with the Aboriginals in 2001), and one on PBS in January 1996 at the start of the American presidential primary season. Ten have been local or regional in the U.S.—eight on "Integrated Resource Planning" for electric utilities in and around Texas, one on educational issues with the Nike Foundation in Oregon, and, most recently, one involving a "Regional Dialogue" on economic cooperation between city and suburbs in New Haven, Connecticut.[7]

Here are some summary observations about Deliberative Polling, as we judge it thus far, from those projects for which we have completed detailed data analysis. First, in every case, we have managed to gather a highly representative sample of the population in question to come for an extended face-to-face deliberation. We can judge the representativeness of the sample by comparing the people who come with those who do not. Since we only invite people after they have taken a conventional survey, we can compare the participants with the nonparticipants both attitudinally and demographically. We can also, of course, compare the participants demographically to census data.

Second, in every case, there are changes of opinion on politics and policy, often quite large changes. For the most part, the considered judgments revealed by Deliberative Polling differ significantly from the respondents' initial responses.

Third, we can demonstrate that the respondents became much more informed by the end of the process, based on information questions asked before and after.

Fourth, we have found, through further analysis, that information gain explains a lot of the opinion change. It is primarily those who become more informed on the issues who also change their views about them.

Fifth, change of opinion in the Deliberative Poll does not systematically correlate with any of the standard sociodemographic factors, such as education, income, class, and gender. Virtually everyone seems capable of deliberating.

Sixth, in cases where there are ranking questions, we have found a higher degree of preference structuration, making cycles less likely after deliberation. In other words, a higher percentage of the sample has single peaked preferences. Respondents may not agree on a single answer, but they agree about what they are agreeing—or disagreeing—about. Deliberation creates a shared space for public opinion.[8]

Seventh, we have not found the debilitating patterns of group "polarization" that have recently been alleged by Cass Sunstein and others to be a necessary artifact of the deliberative process.[9] Unlike jury discussions, our deliberative process does not require an agreed verdict, and it has, with trained moderators, elements of balance that seem to inoculate participants from reaching conclusions as a predictable artifact of the initial group composition.

There are some other key results as well, but the findings above should suffice to fill out the picture of a deliberative consultation that plausibly represents the entire public, in microcosm, under conditions where it can think seriously about the issue in question.

A great deal depends on the good conditions that facilitate the sample becoming more informed on the issue in question. Respondents, knowing that they are to participate in a visible (usually televised) event, begin, from the moment they are asked, to discuss the issue with friends and family and to become more attentive consumers of the media. We view this information effect in anticipation of the event as part of the experimental treatment. However, the learning that respondents do in anticipation is likely to be unbalanced. The respondent when talking to friends and family is likely to talk with people who have similar opinions and who come from similar social locations. The diversity that facilitates balanced deliberation can be furthered in the environment of the Deliberative Poll with balanced briefing documents, balanced panels and random assignment to small groups with trained moderators. For example, in Denmark, in the Deliberative Poll regarding the euro, we happened to have some information questions that specifically identified facts supporting either the "yes" case or the "no" case. In the period leading up to the Deliberative Poll, yes-supporting respondents learned the yes facts but not the no facts; no-supporting respondents learned the no facts but not the yes facts. However, after the weekend of face-to-face deliberation, the gap closed.[10]

After the respondent agrees to participate in the Deliberative Poll, he or she is sent a carefully balanced briefing document on the issue. The document, which is also made available to the press and observers and which is sometimes posted on the Web to help inform other citizens, is meant to offer a reasonably accessible digest of competing arguments and relevant facts on the issue to be deliberated. It is meant to provide a starting point for the discussions on the weekend. Typically, it is vetted by an advisory board of stakeholders on the issue who scrutinize it for balance and accuracy. It is also useful if the same advisory board supervises the selection of competing experts and politicians who answer questions from the sample on the weekend.

When the respondents arrive, they are randomly assigned to small groups that meet with trained moderators. The groups discuss the issue, initially on the basis of the briefing document, and clarify key questions that they wish to ask in plenary sessions with panels of competing experts and, usually later in the weekend, panels of competing politicians or decision makers. In the larger sessions, the experts and politicians do not give speeches. They only respond to questions from the sample. The weekend gathering, which usually meets from Friday evening until midday Sunday, alternates the small group and large group sessions until, at the end of the weekend, the participants respond to the same questionnaire as the one they answered on first contact.[11] At the same time, the television partner has either been broadcasting the large group sessions live or has been taping and editing the proceedings, usually including the small group discussions, for later broadcast. The Deliberative Poll has been called "a poll with a human face" because it puts a human face—and a human voice—on the process of informed opinion change. The weekend combines some of the qualitative characteristics of focus groups or discussion groups with the possibility of studying the opinion changes quantitatively at the individual level.

In sum, the basic idea has proven eminently practical. We use social science to gather a representative microcosm and then facilitate its deliberation under favorable conditions. Ideally, all citizens would participate, but under normal conditions, citizens in mass society are not effectively motivated to do so, for reasons we have already discussed. Hence, the idea is to engage a microcosm, in a good social science experiment, and then use that to represent what informed public opinion would be like—to fellow citizens, to policymakers and to politicians. The considered judgments of the microcosm offer a basis for an informed and representative public voice.

The process produces several different outputs. The most obvious is the before-and-after questionnaire responses—the net opinion changes. These are made available to the media and are usually part of the television broadcast. A second output is more qualitative. The small group discussions, as well as the questions in the plenary sessions, provide a public voice that can be caught in qualitative as well as in quantitative form—through taped and edited accounts of the small group discussions for broadcast, through qualitative research on the recorded sessions, and through observation by decision makers. A third key output is the effect on experts and decision makers who participate. We have found that many policymakers are surprised by the serious engagement and knowledge levels of ordinary citizens as they participate in the process. Deliberative citizens offer a useful contrast to the self-selected intense groups and lobbyists who tend to dominate "town meetings" and similar open forums. A fourth key output is the effect on the mass public who watch the broadcasts. In some cases, such as the Deliberative Poll before the 1999 Australian referendum, we can see from various polls that the broadcasts and newspaper articles had a significant effect.

Studying the effects of these outputs is a complex process. In one series of cases, however, we can clearly see results. In Texas, we conducted a series of Deliberative Polls on "integrated resource planning" for the regulated public utilities of the state. The utilities were required by state law to consult the public and to take account of those consultations in the plans they submitted to the Texas Public Utility Commission (PUC) for how they were going to provide electricity in their service territories in the future. In conjunction with the PUC and with advisory committees representing all the key stakeholders, we conducted Deliberative Polls for all eight investor-owned utilities in the state. The commissioners participated in the Deliberative Polls, responding themselves to questions from the sample at the end of the proceedings. Their enthusiasm for the process, expressed during the process and on the broadcasts, made it clear to everyone that they were going to take the results seriously. And based on the results of the Deliberative Polls, they implemented plans that yielded the largest investments in renewable-energy in the history of the state. Later the legislature, when it deregulated the utility industry, used the results of the Deliberative Poll to justify including a substantial renewable-energy portfolio in the legislation.

I have been asked, does this lead to better public policy? It depends, of course, on your criteria for "better" and to what the Deliberative Poll's results are compared. If it is compared to the advice of experts, then it is certainly arguable that experts are vastly more informed than even our "informed" citizens. However, there are issues of value tradeoffs—namely, of what distributions of benefits and burdens the public is willing to live with. In essence, these are questions of collective political will. Such questions are suitable for public consultation because it is the public that will have to live with the results and finance the expenditures of one policy choice or another.

My position is that if democratic theory suggests an issue is appropriate for public consultation, then deliberative polling is the best practical method available. Compared to all its rivals, it combines political equality (achieved via random sampling) and deliberation to a high degree. Top-of-the-head polls embody a form of political equality but combine it with uninformed opinion. Focus groups offer depth but are too small to employ random sampling or to be representative. Self-selected forums such as "town meetings" are typically dominated by those who feel intensely or can be mobilized to participate. Other deliberative forums, such as the consensus conference or the citizens' jury, are both too small to be representative and push consensus by their decision-making structure. Soliciting opinions in confidential questionnaires, however, finds whatever consensus or genuine opinion change may occur through deliberation, without subjecting participants to the social pressures that can produce a false consensus. For all of these reasons, I believe that if public policymakers are interested in the informed and representative voice of the people on a given issue, then this method, or something very much like it, offers the most credible and practical alternative.

In their landmark study of political participation, Verba, Schlozman, and Brady posit a fundamental criterion that they call "participatory distortion," which "exists when any group of activists—such as protesters, voters or contributors—is unrepresentative of the public with respect to some politically relevant characteristics." Their concern is that "unequal participation has consequences for what is communicated to the government . . . the voices that speak loudly articulate a different set of messages about the state of the public, its needs and its preferences." Almost in passing, they note that this problem would only be solved "were everyone equally active, or were activists drawn at random from across the population."[12] They then leave this apparently utopian counterfactual in order to model the actual state of inequality.

In real life, the very notion of activists drawn at random is oxymoronic, as activists are usually thought of as those who select themselves because they are especially interested, for one reason or another. But in an experiment,[13] we can see what such a world would look like, drawing participants equally from all segments of the population through random sampling. At least for the question at issue, we can see what a world without "participatory distortion" would look like. But Deliberative Polling goes even further, because it combines political equality with deliberation. It attempts to apply political equality not just to participation in a political event, but also through deliberation, to preference formation on the issue in question. If, as Verba, Schlozman, and Brady note, participatory distortion gives government officials a skewed notion of the public voice, then the addition of Deliberative Polling to the public dialogue can serve a constructive purpose.

In Deliberative Polls, we have participants who are not trying to get reelected and who are not ambitious to manipulate the process for personal benefit. When ordinary citizens deliberate, they conscientiously consider the public's problems and, in doing so, they exhibit very much the behavior that Madison sought for the filter. Deliberating citizens show little or no interest in taking away the rights of other citizens or in pursuing merely personal interests at the expense of others. In fact, they show a willingness to make at least modest sacrifices of self-interest for the public good.[14] Madison saw that deliberation was unlikely to produce factions supporting tyranny of the majority. He was right.

Deliberative Polling offers a glimpse of democratic possibilities. It can enrich the public voice as an alternative to top-of-the-head polls. It can serve an advisory function to government officials and legislators if they are interested in what their constituents might think about an issue when more informed. And it embodies a research program exploring what public opinion might be like if the public were motivated to behave a bit more like ideal citizens. At this stage, it is a melding of social science with normative concerns in order to contribute to the public dialogue. Whether, or in what context, we might go further in institutionalizing it is very much an open question awaiting the results of further research.

Notes

1. Madison, "*Federalist* No.10," p. 126.

2. Gallup, *Public Opinion in a Democracy,* p. 15.

3. For a good overview on the state of the public's knowledge, see Delli Carpini and Keeter, *What the American Public Knows and Why It Matters*. For the effects of policy-specific knowledge see Gilens, "Political Ignorance and Collective Policy Preferences."

4. Downs, *An Economic Theory of Democracy*.

5 Converse, "The Nature of Belief Systems." There is a vast literature since, but it has not changed the relevance of the basic insight.

6. It is not quite unique in this dual aspiration. The "choice questionnaire" attempts to provide random samples with more information, but only in the context of the survey process itself. This is a much more modest intervention than a weekend of discussion. Another strategy, Televote, sends respondents a briefing document after a telephone survey and then calls them back at a later time. This strategy also achieves far more modest opinion changes than the Deliberative Poll and probably suffers from the problems discussed here with imbalanced information when people are just stimulated to talk more about an issue at home. Hence it seems fair to say that the Deliberative Poll, while not unique, is clearly the most ambitious effort thus far to achieve these two goals—deliberative or more informed opinion from a scientific random sample. For more on the choice questionnaire, see Neijens, *Choice Questionnaire*. For more on Televote, see Slaton, *Televote*.

7. For an overview of the process and its rationale, see Fishkin, *Voice of the People*. For a detailed analysis of the first Deliberative Poll, see Luskin and Fishkin, "Considered Opinions."

8. List et al., "Can Deliberation Induce Greater Preference Structuration?"

9. Sunstein, "Deliberative Trouble?"

10. Hansen and Andersen, "The Deliberative Poll."

11. On some occasions, there have also been intermediate waves of the questionnaire, to help determine the effects of different portions of the treatment. In Denmark, questions were posed on arrival as well as at the end of the weekend to assess the effect of learning before the weekend. In New Haven, there was an intermediate wave after a random half of the sample had discussed one of two issues but not the other. This permitted us to assess the effects of discussion by comparing those who had discussed a given issue with those who had not.

12. Verba, Schlozman, and Brady, *Voice and Equality*, pp. 11, 15.

13. Strictly speaking, the Deliberative Polls have, at best, been "quasi-experiments" conforming to the "posttest-only" design recommended by Campbell and Stanley in *Experimental and Quasi-Experimental Designs for Research*.

14. For example, in the eight Deliberative Polls held on electric utility matters, the participants consistently showed a dramatically increased willingness to pay more on their monthly utility bills if it would help the environment through alternative energy sources (wind and solar power) or investments in conservation or if it would help poor customers.

9

Polling in a Robust Democracy

Michael A. Genovese
and
Matthew J. Streb

A robust democracy requires an active, enlightened citizenry; free elections; equal access to the halls of power; equal power for all citizens (regardless of income, education, religion, race, or gender); open political institutions; and effective public officials.

History suggests that democracies can be fragile and unstable. Dictatorships can be more efficient. The demands that a robust democracy places upon its citizens can be onerous. The deliberation and debate, consensus and coalition building characteristic of democracies can cause delay and gridlock, frustration and apathy. Pressure to, in the words of businessman-turned-presidential-candidate H. Ross Perot, run government "like a business" puts government on the defensive. In short, democracy isn't easy!

Because of the essential role of the public in a democracy, many argue that polls are extremely important to keep democracy strong. This contention is quite controversial, however. The essays in this book have attempted to unravel some of the mystery embedded in this debate. Certainly not all of the questions regarding polling and democracy have been touched upon; to address them all would require several volumes. Yet we have tried to shed some light on the subject by addressing two broad questions. First, how do—and how should—politicians, specifically the president, use polls? Second, how do these polls affect the public (and democracy)? In short, do polls strengthen or threaten democracy? Do polls strengthen democracy by giving the people a voice and elected officials an idea of public sentiment, or do they undermine democracy by providing faulty information, manipulating the very public opinion that polls are designed to measure, and thereby influence, in a dangerous way, politics and election outcomes?

The President, the Public, and Democratic Theory

The president serves a variety of functions for the American public. The political scientist Fred Greenstein summarizes the psychological connections between the president and the people, noting that to the people, the president serves (1) as a symbol of national unity, stability, and the American way of life; (2) as an outlet for affect, for feeling good about America; (3) as a cognitive aid, simplifying complexity into a single symbol; and (4) as a means of vicarious participation in the political world.[1]

Because the president serves both as head of government (the nation's chief politician) and head of state (the symbolic representation of the nation), he is the chief divider of the nation as well as its chief unifier. Ronald Reagan was a masterful head of state, as evidenced in the aftermath of the *Challenger* disaster, when Reagan took on the role of high priest and national healer for a nation devastated by tragedy. This role, played so well by Reagan, added to his prestige and enabled him at once to reinforce his role as shaman and to rise above politics and become a symbol for the whole nation. Likewise, a beleaguered Bill Clinton, facing a wide range of accusations and investigations, was able, in response to a terrorist attack in Oklahoma City, to serve as national healer and shaman for a grieving nation. Public opinion polls have indicated that George W. Bush has succeeded in this role as well after the September 11th attacks.

Thus, invested in the office of the presidency is high respect, but also high expectations (added to by presidential campaign promises). And yet, as noted in chapter 2, the president's powers are not commensurate with his responsibilities or the public's expectations. This often leads presidents to frustration and also to declines in their popularity. In addition, if the public continues to demand that the government deliver on contradictory expectations (e.g., lower taxes *and* more government services), presidents are put in no-win situations. Given this dilemma, what's a president to do?

Theodore Lowi argues that presidents resolve this dilemma by resorting to rule by political manipulation. Impression management replaces policy achievement. Appearances are everything.[2] It is the president as the Wizard of Oz. The masters of the art of image manipulation were the handlers of Ronald Reagan. True, they had an excellent product to manage, but they masterfully played the media game, offering "pretty pictures" and staged events all designed to put the right spin on the situation. Brace and Hinckley maintain that this excessive reliance on appearances has led to the development of a "public-relations presidency . . . concerned primarily with maintaining and increasing public support."[3] In the *Personal President*, Lowi describes this development as "a plebiscitary republic with a personal presidency."

What is the proper function of the president as leader in our democratic system? Should he follow the public's wishes? Should he attempt to educate the public? Or should he attempt to *act*, to move the government in whatever direction he feels best? Should the president find out what the people want and merely attempt to give it to them? Or should he speak truth (however unpleasant) to power?

The role of leader in a democratic society unveils a web of paradoxes and contradictions that can never be wholly resolved. And while the Founding Fathers feared a president who might fan the embers of popular passions,[4] it is clear that the "democratization"[5] of the presidency has led to the president's becoming the embodiment of the nation's government, making the president serve as a modern "interpreter in chief."[6]

Bruce Miroff writes eloquently of the "tension between leadership and democracy," arguing that for leadership to be democratic, the leader must have

> A respect for followers, rooted in a recognition of what Herman Melville called the "democratic dignity" of every individual. . . . Democratic leaders want for followers what they want for themselves; their goals are egalitarian rather than exclusionary. Committed to the democratic belief in self-government, they understand that leadership must aim at engagement with followers rather than mastery. Yet engagement is a far cry from pandering; to nurture the democratic possibilities of citizenship, democratic leaders must be willing to question, challenge, even defy common conventions. In the face of the conventional antithesis between power and education, democratic leadership raises the possibility that dialogue between leaders and followers can be mutually empowering.[7]

In essence, democratic leadership encompasses a moral vision with egalitarian goals. Democratic leaders question, challenge, and empower citizens. They engage in a dialogue with the people. They are educators.[8]

During his presidency, Jimmy Carter often attempted to educate the people on the limits of America's power, thereby treating the American public with the respect due an educated citizenry in a democracy. But Carter was unable to convince the public that it had to settle for less, make sacrifices, and accept limits. Or perhaps the public refused to listen, refused to believe, and blamed the messenger. This opened the door for Ronald Reagan, who mocked limits and scoffed at sacrifice. He promised the public easy, quick solutions to complex problems. He flattered the public and told them to buy, buy, spend, spend. They did. And at the end of the eight years of the Reagan presidency, the United States went from being the world's largest creditor nation to the world's largest debtor nation. Carter spoke of a tough reality; Reagan offered the public candy. Carter gave the public stagflation; Reagan offered a new approach. Carter lost; Reagan won. In the absence of war, calling for sacrifice seems to be a no-win proposition.[9]

Only by creating a cadre of citizen-leaders can we hope to democratize (and thereby empower) leadership in the United States. But is this possible in the fractious, divisive, and petty politics of left versus right? If the public can be manipulated and misinformed by bogus polls, how can they exercise informed judgment?

Presidents who lead in the democratic spirit create leaders, foster citizen responsibility, and inspire and empower others to assume leadership responsibilities in their communities. Democratic leaders establish a moral vision; pursue egalitarian goals; question, challenge, engage, and educate citizens; offer hope. Emile Zapata said that "strong leaders make a weak people."[10] But strong *democratic leaders* help create *strong citizens*. Eugene Debs captured the dilemma when he said: "Too long have the workers of the world waited for some Moses to lead them out of bondage. He has not come; he will not come. I would not lead you out if I could; for if you would be led out, you could be led back again."[11]

The previous section mentions only the president and his role as a leader in a democratic society. Certainly the president has the greatest leadership responsibilities, but he is not the only elected official who faces the dilemma of paying homage to public opinion while also leading the public. Almost any elected official in a representative democracy is caught in this bind. They are criticized if they pay too much attention to public opinion, but they are voted out of office if they ignore the opinions of the public on important issues—and sometimes it is difficult to determine what those important issues are.[12] In a sense, they are damned if they do and damned if they don't.

Do polls imprison our leaders, or do they liberate them to govern more effectively? In chapter 3, Jacobs and Jackson remind us that voters reach decisions on whom to vote for, not necessarily on the basis of a clear understanding of policy issues, but by employing "less taxing cognitive strategies." Concluding that "instead of policy issues driving voters, research now suggests the electorate relies on personality, character, and personal image."

That being the case, what "calculated strategy" do politicians employ? As Jacobs and Jackson write, "It makes logical and practical sense that ambitious politicians would appeal to voters on the basis of their personal image rather than hard, substantive policy." This puts a premium on a president using sophisticated polling to manipulate voters' perceptions. If image trumps policy, and if the means exist to manipulate the image, of course presidents will be drawn to such a course as they try to maneuver in the complex world of the Madisonian system of check and balances—anything that tips the scale in the favor of a president will be appealing from a White House perspective.

To Jacobs and Jackson, this raises fundamental questions about the nature of a representative government. They ask:

> Is the health of our representative form of government most threatened by citizens struggling to balance a busy life with meaningful democratic participation or by elites intent on enacting the ideological agendas that they and their financial and party supporters favor? Put simply, are the strategies of political elites endangering the health of a vibrant representative government?

Here Diane Heith enters the debate. Arguing that polling techniques drive presidents to the "permanent campaign," Heith asks, "Does the incorporation of polling produce permanent campaign leadership?" Heith believes it does, arguing that "Polling stands at the heart of the modern, candidate-centered presidential campaign." She concludes that this trend is "ultimately a problem for democracy," going so far as to suggest that "This is demagoguery, not democracy."

If, indeed, presidents focus on image to the exclusion of policy, and if the permanent campaign now dominates efforts to govern, then we confront a deep democratic dilemma. Governing is more than image manipulation, more than perpetually campaigning. In a robust democracy, governing is about making choices about how we will live, about where we wish to go, about how we will get there. If our leaders no longer engage us in a democratic debate about possible futures, if they cease to be educators and become more tools of manipulation, then democracy becomes a sham, and presidential "leadership" becomes merely the art of manipulation.

It is not clear that we want politicians to follow public opinion on all issues. While a recent survey indicated that the public believes that politicians should mostly follow the will of the people,[13] there are many issues on which the public is either uninterested or ill-informed, making the trustee model of representation more suitable in these instances. Nor is it clear that politicians themselves are adequately informed on all issues, but in theory, at least, they can obtain information more easily—from colleagues who are informed, government offices, interest groups—than the general public. Even the contributors to this book would not argue that politicians should follow the polls on *all* issues. Nevertheless, polls remain essential so long as a robust democracy obliges our political leaders to follow the expressed will of the people. If a mark of a robust democracy is whether public policy follows public opinion, perhaps somewhat surprisingly numerous studies have indicated, both at the federal and state levels, that American democracy is indeed quite strong.[14]

Polling in a Democratic Society

Questions regarding polls and democracy extend beyond whether politicians should use them. Indeed, polls have a significant effect on several aspects of society—many of which can be quite negative. The media and the public are generally uneducated when it comes to understanding polls. Poll results can be easily manipulated by simply changing the wording of a question or where the question is asked in the course of the survey. Journalists are rarely trained in interpreting poll results or distinguishing between a good poll and a bad one. They tend to merely accept the validity of a poll and ask few questions. The media may report information as fact that is wrong, and thereby influence public perceptions. As Traugott illustrated in chapter 5, the media may interpret the results of the same poll in very different ways. And as Wright noted in chapter 7, the media, in their pursuit of viewers, can make a premature call on election night.

The public is also generally unable to distinguish between properly constructed and poorly constructed polls. Too often, the public takes the results of polls as fact without really investigating how the poll was conducted. In fairness to the public, it is not always easy to learn how a poll was implemented, especially when virtually all that is reported are poll results. To understand whether a poll is valid, you must know many things, such as how the pollster chose the sample, the margin of error, the question wording, and the question order.

The fact that so many "pseudo polls" are conducted today also raises questions about the role of polling in a democracy. As Streb and Pinkus argued in chapter 6, push polls and other types of unscientific polling practices can distort true public opinion and make the public become cynical not only about survey research, but about politics in general. Even the results of scientific polls are often questioned because of the presence of "non-attitudes" as Fishkin noted in chapter 8. Clearly then, one must read polls results with caution.

Conclusion

All of this leads us back to our initial question: Do polls help or hinder democracy? The general consensus of the authors in the book is that polling does indeed play an important role in a democratic society. Even Fishkin, who provides the most stinging critique of traditional polling, believes that polls play a central role in a democracy. As Traugott argues, polls give the public a voice and a sense that their voice matters. They can present politicians with the will of the people, which helps the politicians govern more effectively. They help candidates develop campaign strategy and test whether that strategy is effective. And, as Wright makes clear, they provide researchers and analysts with useful and important information about phenomena that we otherwise would have great difficulty understanding. Certainly no one is arguing that democracy cannot exist without polling—it did so quite well in America for more than one hundred years without scientific polling—but polls can help create a stronger, more robust democracy.

That being said, the general consensus is also one of extreme caution. Whether we like it or not, polls are here to stay. The question then is whether they are to be an asset to democracy or a liability. When used properly and when their limitations are understood, polls add to the strengths and legitimacy of democracies. But, as Streb and Pinkus argue, when used improperly, polls and pseudo polls can undermine democracy. They can be tools of single-issue advocates, monied interests, unethical pollsters, and unscrupulous politicians in their efforts to manipulate public attitudes and undermine democratic viability.

However, the problems of polling should not make us disregard polling or the importance of its place in a democracy. Instead, we must work harder to inform the media and the public about polling practices. An informed public will lessen many of the previously mentioned problems with polling. By no means is this task an easy one, but it is certainly one that is worth the effort. As we said, democracy can exist without polls, but they are here to stay. Therefore, we must find ways to use polls in proper ways and help politicians, the media, and the public realize polling's inherent strengths and weaknesses.

Notes

1. Greenstein, "What the President Means to Americans," pp. 130–31.

2. Lowi, *Personal President*.

3. Brace and Hinckley, *Follow the Leader*, p. 1.

4. Tulis, *Rhetorical Presidency*.

5. Pfiffner, *Modern Presidency*.

6. Stuckey, *President as Interpreter-in-Chief*.

7. Miroff, *Icons of Democracy*, p. 2.

8. Cronin, "Leadership and Democracy"; Barber, "Neither Leaders nor Followers."

9. Genovese, *Presidency in an Age of Limits*.

10. Barber, "Neither Leaders nor Followers," p. 117.

11. Kann, "Challenging Lockean Liberalism in America," p. 214.

12. Arnold, *Logic of Congressional Action*.

13. Morin, "Unconventional Wisdom."

14. Stimson, Mackuen, and Erikson, "Dynamic Representation"; Bartels, "Constituency Opinion and Congressional Policy Making"; De Boef and Stimson, "The Dynamic Structure of Congressional Elections"; Erikson, Wright, and McIver, *Statehouse Democracy*; Erikson and Wright, "Voters, Candidates, and Issues in Congressional Elections."

References

Alvarez, Michael. *Information and Elections*. Ann Arbor: University of Michigan Press, 1997.

Arnold, R. Douglas. *The Logic of Congressional Action*. New Haven: Yale University Press, 1990.

Asher, Herbert. *Polling and the Public: What Every Citizen Should Know*, 4th ed. Washington, D.C.: CQ Press, 1998.

———. *Polling and the Public: What Every Citizen Should Know*, 5th ed. Washington, D.C.: CQ Press, 2001.

"At a Glance—Pointed Questions." *The New York Times*, 14 February 2000, A16.

Balz, Dan. "Partisan Divisions Bedevil Bush; Advisors Seek Ways to Redefine Presidency as Popularity Slips." *Washington Post*, 1 July 2001, A01.

Barber, Benjamin. "Neither Leaders nor Followers." In *Essays in Honor of James MacGregor Burns*, ed. Michael R. Beschloss, and Thomas E. Cronin. Englewood Cliffs, N.J.: Prentice-Hall, 1989.

Bartels, Larry. "Consituency Opinion and Congressional Policy Making: The Reagan Defense Buildup." *American Political Science Review* 85 (1991): 457–74.

Beal, Richard S., and Ronald H. Hinckley. "Presidential Decision Making and Public Opinion Polls." *Annals, AAPS* 472 (1984): 72–84.

Berlo, David, James Lemert, and Robert Mertz. "Dimensions for Evaluating the Acceptability of Message Sources." *Public Opinion Quarterly*, 33 (1969): 563–76.

Black, Duncan. *The Theory of Committees and Elections*. Cambridge: Cambridge University Press, 1958.

Blumenthal, Sidney. *The Permanent Campaign: Inside the World of Elite Political Operatives*. New York: Beacon Press, 1980.

Blumer, Herbert. "Public Opinion and Public Opinion Polling." *American Sociological Review* 13 (1948): 542–54.

Bogart, Leo. "Politics, Polls, and Poltergeists." *Society* 35 (1998): 4.

Bonafede, Dom. "A Pollster to the President, Wirthlin Is Where the Action Is." *National Journal*, 12 December 1981: 2184–88.

Brace, Paul, and Barbara Hinckley. *Follow the Leader: Opinion Polls and the Modern Presidents*. New York: Basic Books, 1992.

Brady, Henry E., Michael C. Herron, Walter R. Mebane, Jr., Jasjeet Singh Sekhon, Kenneth W. Shotts, and Jonathan Wand. "Law and Data: The Butterfly Ballot Episode." *PS* 34 (2000): 59–70.

Braxton, Greg. "TV's Early Call in Arizona Vote Angers Dole." *Los Angeles Times*, 29 February 1996, F1.

Brice, Arthur. "'Not a Single Time. Never.' President Passionate in Denying Allegations." *The Atlanta Journal and Constitution*, 27 January 1998, A1.

Brody, Richard A. *Assessing the President: The Media, Elite Opinion, and Public Support*. Stanford, Calif.: Stanford University Press, 1991.

Bryce, James. *The American Commonwealth*. New York: Macmillan, 1988.

Bull, John M. R. "Bill Would Prohibit Biased Phone Calls." *Pittsburgh Post-Gazette*, 14 September 2001, C-10.

Bumiller, Susan. "Giuliani Accuses Mrs. Clinton of Negative Calls, Disguised as Polling." *The New York Times*, 23 February 2000, B6.

Campbell, Andrea, and Bradley Palmquist. "Exit Polls as a Source of Political Data." Paper presented at the annual meeting of the American Political Science Association, Boston, 3–6 September 1998.

Campbell, Angus, Phillip E. Converse, Warren E. Miller, and Donald E. Stokes. *The American Voter*. New York: Wiley, 1960.

Campbell, Donald, and Julian Stanley. *Experimental and Quasi-Experimental Designs for Research*. Boston: Houghton Mifflin, 1963.

Cantril, Albert H. *The Opinion Connection*. Washington, D.C.: CQ Press, 1991.

Cardwell, Diane. "Badillo Accuses Bloomberg of Conducting Smear Campaign in Mayor's Race." *The New York Times*, 4 July 2001, B4.

Ceci, Stephen J., and Edward L. Kain. "Jumping on the Bandwagon with the Underdog: The Impact of Attitude Polls on Polling Behavior." *Public Opinion Quarterly*, 46 (1982): 228–42.

Center for Responsive Politics. "All Presidential Candidates" 2002. Accessed 21 June <www.opensecrets.org>.

Clymer, Adam. "A Bush Campaign Chief Who Knows Questions." *The New York Times*, 8 December 1991, 34.

"CNN Announces Election Night Coverage Change Following 'Debacle.'" Accessed 14 February 2001. <www.cnn.com/2001/ALLPOLITICS/stories/02/02/cnn.report>.

Cohen, Richard E. *Changing Course in Washington: Clinton and the New Congress*. New York: Macmillan College Publishing Company, 1994.

Collins, Monica. "Eye on the Media: The Most Accurate Call of All." *The Boston Herald,* 9 November 2000, A60.

———. "Television a Picture of Shame—Some Soul-searching Needed." *The Boston Herald,* 9 November 2000, A22.

Connolly, Francis J., and Charley Manning. "What 'Push Polling' Is and What It Isn't." *The Boston Globe*, 16 August 2001, A21.

Converse, Jean M., and Stanley Presser. *Survey Questions: Handcrafting the Standardized Questionnaire*. Beverly Hills, Calif.: Sage Publications, 1996.

Converse, Philip E. "The Nature of Belief Systems in Mass Publics." In *Ideology and Discontent*, ed. David E. Apter. New York: Free Press, 1964.

———. "Attitudes and Non-attitudes: Continuation of a Dialogue." In *The Quantitative Analysis of Social Problems*, ed. Edward R. Tufte. Reading, Mass.: Addison-Wesley, 1970.

———. "Changing Conceptions of Public Opinion in the Political Process." *Public Opinion Quarterly* 51 (1987): S12–S24.

Cronin, Thomas E. "Leadership and Democracy." *Liberal Education* 73 (1987): 36.

Crossley, Archibald M. "Straw Polls in 1936." *Public Opinion Quarterly* 1 (1937): 24–35.

Dalton, Russell J. "Political Parties and Political Representation: Party Supports and Party Elites in Nine Nations." *Comparative Political Studies* 18 (1985): 267–99.

Daves, Rob. "Push Polling Controversy Muddies the Field for Public Opinion Surveyors." *The Star Tribune*, 17 February 2000: 28A.

Dawson, Anne. "Day Accused of Playing Dirty Poll Ploy Would Discourage Voting." *The Toronto Sun*, 17 June 2000, 3.

De Boef, Suzanna, and James A. Stimson. "The Dynamic Structure of Congressional Elections." *Journal of Politics* 57 (1995): 630–48.

Delli Carpini, Michael X., and Scott Keeter. *What the American Public Knows and Why It Matters*. New Haven: Yale University Press, 1996.

Denwoodie, Robbie. "Democracy the Loser in TV Poll Dramas." *The Herald-Glascow*, 9 November 2000, 15.

Disch, Lisa. "Publicity-Stunt Participation and Sound Bite Polemics: The Health Care Debate, 1993–94." *The Journal of Health Politics, Policy, and Law* 21 (1996): 3–34.

Downs, Anthony. *An Economic Theory of Democracy*. New York: Harper and Row, 1957.

Dran, Ellen M., and Ann Hildreth. "What the Public Thinks about How We Know What It Is Thinking." *International Journal of Public Opinion Research* 7 (1995): 128–44.

Edsall, Thomas. "Confrontation Is the Key to Clinton's Popularity; Adviser Morris's Strategy Proves Inconsistent." *The Washington Post*, 24 December 1995, A06.

Edwards, George. *The Public Presidency*. New York: St. Martin Press, 1983.

———. "Frustration and Folly: Bill Clinton and the Public Presidency." In *The Clinton Presidency: First Appraisals*, ed. Colin Campbell and Bert Rockman. Chatham, N.J.: Chatham House, 1996.

———. "Campaigning Is Not Governing: Bill Clinton's Rhetorical Presidency." In *The Clinton Legacy*, ed. Colin Campbell and Bert Rockman. New York: Chatham House, 2000.

Eisinger, Robert. "Gauging Public Opinion in the Hoover White House: Understanding the Roots of Presidential Polling." *Presidential Studies Quarterly* 30 (2000): 643–61.

Epstein, Laurily, and Gerald Strom. "Survey Research and Election Night Projections." *Public Opinion* 7 (1984): 48–50.

Erikson, Robert S., and Christopher Wlezien. "The Timeline of Political Campaigns." Paper presented at the annual meeting of the American Political Science Association, Boston, 3–6 September 1998.

Erikson, Robert S., and Gerald C. Wright. "Voters, Candidates, and Issues in Congressional Elections." In *Congress Reconsidered*, ed. Lawrence C. Dodd and Bruce I. Oppenheimer 7th ed. Washington, D.C.: CQ Press, 2001.

Erikson, Robert S., Gerald C. Wright, and John P. McIver. 1993. *Statehouse Democracy: Public Opinion and Policy in the American States*. Cambridge: Cambridge University Press.

"Exit Polls, Stage Left." *Christian Science Monitor*, 8 December 2000, 10.

Fishkin, James S. *Voice of the People: Public Opinion and Democracy*. New Haven: Yale University Press, 1997.

Fleitas, Daniel W. "Bandwagon and Underdog Effects in Minimal-Information Elections." *American Political Science Review* 65 (1971): 434–38.

Fox, Jonathan S. "Push Polling: The Art of Political Persuasion." *Florida Law Review*, 1997, 563–628.

Freisma, H. Paul, and Ronald D. Hedlund. "The Reality of Representational Roles." In *Public Opinion and Public Policy*, ed. Norman R. Luttbeg Itasca, Ill.: Peacock, 1981.

Fritz, Sarah. "As Bush Sinks in Polls He Tries New Directions." *St. Petersburg Times*, 2 July 2002, A1.

Gallup, George. *Public Opinion in a Democracy*. Princeton, N.J.: Princeton University Press, 1939.

Gallup, George, and Saul Rae. *The Pulse of Democracy.* New York: Simon and Schuster, 1940.

Gawiser, Sheldon R., and G. Evans Witt. *A Journalist's Guide to Public Opinion Polls*. Westport, Conn.: Praeger, 1994.

Genovese, Michael A. *The Presidency and the Age of Limits*. Westport, Conn.: Greenwood, 1993.

———. *The Presidential Dilemma: Leadership in the American System.* New York: Harper Collins, 1999.

———. *The Power of the American Presidency, 1789–2000.* New York: Oxford University Press, 2001.

Gilens, Martin. "Political Ignorance and Collective Policy Preferences." *American Political Science Review* 95 (2001): 379–96.

Ginsberg, Benjamin. "How Polling Transforms Public Opinion." In *Manipulating Public Opinion*, ed. Michael Margolis and Gary A. Mauser. Pacific Grove, Calif.: Brooks/Cole Publishing Company, 1989.

Gitlin, Todd. "Oops, I'll Say It Again." *The Observer,* 12 November 2000, 13.

Goidel, Robert K., and Todd G. Shields. "The Vanishing Marginals, the Bandwagon, and the Mass Media." *The Journal of Politics* 56 (1994): 802–10.

Goldman, Eric F. "Poll on the Polls." *Public Opinion Quarterly* 8(1944): 461–67.

Goyder, John. "Surveys on Surveys: Limitations and Potentialities." *Public Opinion Quarterly* 50(1986): 27–41.

Greenstein, Fred. "What the President Means to the Americans." In *Choosing the President*, ed. James David Barber. New York: American Assembly, 1974.

Grofman, Bernard, Robert Griffin, and Amitai Glazer. "Identical Geography, Different Party: A Natural Experiment on the Magnitude of Party Differences in the U.S. Senate, 1960–84." In *Developments in Electoral Geography*, ed. R. J. Johnston, F. M. Shelley, and P. J. Taylor. New York: Routledge, 1990.

Guarino, David R. "'Push Poll' Firm IDs Client." *The Boston Herald*, 11 August 2001, A5.

———. "'Push Pollsters' in 9th Implicated Elsewhere." *The Boston Herald*, 13 August 2001, A3.

Haldeman, H. R. *The Haldeman Diaries: Inside the Nixon White House*. New York: G. P. Putnam, 1994.

Hansen, Kasper, and Vibeke Normann Andersen. "The Deliberative Poll: Opinion Formation in Experimental Context of Deliberative Polling." Paper presented at the annual meeting of the American Political Science Association, San Francisco, 30 August–2 September 2001.

Hart, Roderick. *The Sound of Leadership*. Chicago: University of Chicago Press, 1997.

Heclo, Hugh. "Campaigning and Governing a Conspectus." In *The Permanent Campaign and Its Future*, ed. Norman Ornstein and Thomas Mann. Washington, D.C.: The Brookings Institution, 2000.

Heith, Diane J. "The Clinton Health Plan: Historical Perspective." *Health Affairs* 14(1995): 86–98.

———. "Polling for Policy: Public Opinion and Presidential Leadership." Ph.D. diss., Brown University, 1997.

———. "Staffing the White House Public Opinion Apparatus: 1969–1988." *Public Opinion Quarterly* 63(1998): 162–89.

———. "Polling for a Defense: The White House Public Opinion Apparatus and the Clinton Impeachment." *Presidential Studies Quarterly* 30(2000): 783–90.

———. "Presidential Polling and the Potential for Leadership." In *Presidential Power: Forging the Presidency for the Twenty-First Century*, ed. Lawrence R. Jacobs, Martha Kumar, and Robert Shapiro. New York: Columbia University Press, 2000.

Hickley, Neil. "The Big Mistake." *Columbia Journalism Review*, January/February, 2001.

Hippler, Hans J., and Norbert Schwarz. "'No-Opinion' Filters: A Cognitive Perspective." *International Journal of Public Opinion Research* 1(1989): 77–87.

Holmberg, Soren. "Political Representation in Sweden." *Scandinavian Political Studies,* 12(1989): 1–36.

House of Representatives Home Page. Accessed 22 March 2002. <www.house.gov>. "Push Poll Disclaimer Act." H. R. 248. 105th Congress.

Inglehart, Ronald. "The Changing Structure of Political Cleavages in Western Society." In *Electoral Change in Advanced Industrial Democracies: Realignment or Dealignment?*, ed. Russell J. Dalton, Scott Flanagan, and Paul Allen Beck. Princeton: Princeton University Press, 1984.

Jackson, John. "Election Night Reporting and Voter Turnout." *American Journal of Political Science* 27(1983): 615–35.

Jacobs, Lawrence R. "A Social Interpretation of Institutional Change: Public Opinion and Policy Making in the Enactment of the British National Health Service Act of 1946 and the American Medicare Act of 1965." Ph.D. diss., Columbia University, 1990.

———. "The Recoil Effect: Public Opinion and Policymaking in the U.S. and Britain." *Comparative Politics* 24(1992): 199–217.

———. "Institutions and Culture: Health Policy and Public Opinion in the U.S. and Britain." *World Politics* 44(1992): 179–209.

———. *The Health of Nations: Public Opinion and the Making of Health Policy in the U.S. and Britain*. Ithaca: Cornell University Press, 1993.

———. "Politics of America's Supply State: Health Reform and Technology." *Health Affairs* 14(1995): 143–57.

———. "The Presidency and the Press: The Paradox of the White House 'Communications War.'" In *The Presidency and the Political System*, ed. Michael Nelson. 7th ed. Washington, D.C.: Congressional Quarterly Press, 2002.

Jacobs, Lawrence R., Hanes Druckman, and Eric Ostermeier. "A Political Theory of Candidate Strategy: Nixon's Use of Polling Information on Policy Issues and Candidate Image." (Typescript 2002.).

Jacobs, Lawrence R., and Melinda Jackson. "Reconciling the Influence of Policy Issues and Candidate Image on Election Campaigns: The Private Polling and Campaign Strategy of the Nixon White House." Paper presented at the annual meeting of the American Political Science Association, Washington, D.C., 31 August–3 September 2000.

Jacobs, Lawrence R., and Robert Y. Shapiro. "Public Decisions, Private Polls: John F. Kennedy's Presidency." Paper presented at the annual meeting of the Midwest Political Science Association, Chicago, 9–11 April 1992.

———. "Issues, Candidate Image, and Priming: The Use of Private Polls in Kennedy's 1960 Presidential Campaign." *American Political Science Review* 88(1994): 527–40.

———. "The Rise of Presidential Polling: The Nixon White House in Historical Perspective." *Public Opinion Quarterly* 59(1995): 163–95.

———. *Politicians Don't Pander: Political Manipulation and the Loss of Democratic Responsiveness*. Chicago: University of Chicago Press, 2000.

Jacobs, Lawrence R., and Robert Y. Shapiro. *Politicians Don't Pander: Political Manipulation and the Loss of Democratic Responsiveness*. Chicago: University of Chicago Press, 2000.

Jamieson, Kathleen Hall, and Paul Waldman. "The Morning After: The Effect of the Network Call for Bush." *Political Communication* 19(2000): 113–18.

Jones, Randall J., Jr. *Who Will Be in the White House? Predicting Presidential Elections*. New York: Longman, 2002.

Kang, Mee-Eun, Paul Lavrakas, Stanley Presser, Vincent Price, and Michael Traugott. "Public Interest in Polling." Paper presented at the annual meeting of the American Association for Public Opinion Research, St. Louis, 15–17 May 1998.

Kann, Mark E. "Challenging Lockean Liberalism in America." *Political Theory* 8(1980): 203–22.

Kernell, Samuel. *Going Public*. Washington, D.C.: CQ Press, 1986.

Killian, Linda. *The Freshman: What Happened to the Republican Revolution*. Boulder, Colo.: Westview Press, 1998.

Kinder, Donald, and David O. Sears. "Public Opinion and Political Action." In vol. 2 of *The Handbook of Social Psychology*, ed. Gardner Lindzey and Elliot Aronson 3rd ed. New York: Random House, 1985.

King, Gary, and Lyn Ragsdale. *The Elusive Executive*. Washington, D.C.: CQ Press, 1988.

Konner, Joan, James Risser, and Ben Wattenberg. "Television's Performance on Election Night 2000: A Report for CNN." Accessed 29 January 2001. <www.cnn.com/2001/ALLPOLITICS/stories/02/02/ cnn.report.cnn.pdf>.

Krosnick, Jon A. "Question Wording and Reports of Survey Results: The Case of Louis Harris and Associates and Aetna Life and Casualty." *Public Opinion Quarterly,* 53(1989):107–13.

Kuklinski, James H., and Donald J. McCrone. "Electoral Accountability as a Source of Policy Representation." In *Public Opinion and Policy*, ed. Norman R. Luttbeg. Itasca, Ill.: Peacock, 1981.

"Labor Accused of Push Polling." *The Age* (Melbourne), 9 November 2001, 9.

Ladd, Everett Carll. "The Election Polls: An American Waterloo." *Chronicle of Higher Education*, 22 November 1996, A52.

Lau, Richard R. "Political Motivation and Political Cognition." In vol. 2 of *Handbook of Motivation and Cognition: Foundations of Social Behavior*, ed. Richard Sorrentino and E. Tory Huggins New York: Guilford Press, 1990.

Lavrakas, Paul J., Jack K. Holley, and Peter V. Miller. "Public Reactions to Polling during the 1988 Presidential Election Campaign." In *Polling and Presidential Election Coverage*, ed. Paul J. Lavrakas and Jack K. Holley. Newbury Park, Calif.: Sage Publications, 1991.

Lavrakas, Paul J., and Michael W. Traugott. *Election Polls, the News Media, and Democracy*. Chatham, N.J.: Chatham House, 2000.

Lavrakas, Paul J., Michael W. Traugott, and Peter V. Miller, eds. *Presidential Polls and the News Media*. Boulder, Colo.: Westview Press, 1995.

Lichter, S. Robert and Richard E. Noyes. "There They Go Again: Media Coverage of Campaign '96." In *Political Parties, Campaigns, and Elections*, ed. Robert E. DiClerico. Upper Saddle River, N.J.: Prentice-Hall, 2000.

Lincoln, Abraham. "The Gettysburg Address." In *Lincoln on Democracy*, ed. Mario Cuomo and Harold Holzer New York: Harper Collins, 1990.

List, Christian, Iain McLean, James Fishkin, and Robert Luskin. "Can Deliberation Induce Greater Preference Structuration? Evidence from Deliberative Opinion Polls." Paper presented at the annual meeting of the American Political Science Association, Washington, D.C., 31 August–3 September 2000.

Listhaug, Ola, Stuart Macdonald, and George Rabinowitz. "A Comparative Spatial Analysis of European Party Systems." *Scandinavian Political Studies* 13(1990): 227–54.

Lodge, Milton, and Patrick Stroh. "Inside the Mental Voting Booth: An Impression-Driven Process Model of Candidate Evaluation." In *Explorations in Political Psychology*, ed. Shanto Iyengar and James McGuire. Durham, N.C.: Duke University Press, 1993.

Lowi, Theodore J. *The Personal President: Power Invested, Promise Unfulfilled*. Ithaca: Cornell University, 1985.

Lusetich, Robert. "Premature Evaluation—First with the Worst." *The Australian*, 16 November 2000, M01.

Luskin, Robert, and James Fishkin, and Roger Jewell. "Considered Opinions: Deliberative Polling in Britain." *British Journal of Political Science* 32(2002): 32.

MacKuen, Michael B., Robert S. Erikson, and James A. Stimson. "Peasants or Bankers? The American Electorate and the U.S. Economy." *American Political Science Review* 86(1992): 597–611.

Madison, James. "*Federalist* No. 10." In *The Federalist Papers*, by James Madison, Alexander Hamilton, and John Jay. Edited by Isaac Kramnick. New York: Penguin Books, 1987.

Markus, George, and Philip Converse. "A Dynamic Simultaneous Equation Model of Electoral Choice." *American Political Science Review* 73(1979): 1055–70.

McAllister, Bill. "Bush Polls Apart from Clinton in Use of Marketing." *Denver Post*, 17 June 2001, A14.

McInturff, Bill. "Partner, Public Opinion Strategies." 1995. The letter was a follow-up to a push poll speech given at the AAPOR Conference. The letter was circulated to both Democratic and Republican pollsters for their comments and support and then released to the press.

McWilliams, Wilson Carey. "The Meaning of the Election." In *The Election of 2000*, ed. Gerald M. Pomper New York: Chatham House, 2001.

Meyer, Philip. "Stop Pulling Punches with Polls." *Columbia Journalism Review*, November/December, 1991.

Miller, Arthur, Martin Wattenberg, and Oksana Malanchuk. "Schematic Assessments of Presidential Candidates." *American Political Science Review* 80(1986): 521–40.

Miroff, Bruce. *Icons of Democracy.* New York: Basic Books, 1993.

Mitofsky, Warren J. "Fool Me Twice." *Public Perspective*, May/June 2001, 36–38.

———. "How Pollsters and Reporters Can Do a Better Job of Informing the Public: A Challenge for Campaign '96." In *Presidential Polls and News Media*, ed. Paul J. Lavrakas, Michael W. Traugott, and Peter V. Miller. Boulder, Colo.: Westview Press, 1995.

Moon, Nick. *Opinion Polls: History, Theory, and Practice*. New York: Manchester University Press, 1999.

Moore, Robert. *The Superpollsters: How they Measure and Manipulate Public Opinion in America*. New York: Four Walls/Eight Windows, 1992.

Morin, Richard. "Unconventional Wisdom." *The Washington Post,* 21 February 1999, B5.

Morone, James. "The Administration of Health Care Reform." *The Journal of Health Politics, Policy, and Law*, 19(1994): 233–237.

Morris, Dick. *Behind the Oval Office: Getting Reelected against All Odds*. Los Angeles: Renaissance Books, 1999.

———. *The New Prince*. Los Angeles: Renaissance Books, 1999.

———. *Vote.com: How Big-Money Lobbyists and the Media Are Losing Their Influence, and the Internet Is Giving Power to the People.* New York: Renaissance Books, 1999.

Mosier, N., and A. Ahlgren. "Credibility of Precision Journalism." *Journalism Quarterly* 58(1981): 375–81.

Moskowitz, David, and Patrick Stroh. "Expectation-Driven Assessments of Political Candidates." *Political Psychology* 17(1998): 695–712.

Nagourney, Adam, and Dean E. Murphy. "Attack on *Cole* Is Raised as Issue in New York Race." *The New York Times*, 29 October 2000, A1.

National Council on Public Polls. Press release, 22 May 1995.

Navazio, Robert. "An Experimental Approach to Bandwagon Research." *Public Opinion Quarterly*, 41(1977): 217–25.

Neijens, Peter. *The Choice Questionnaire: Design and Evaluation of an Instrument for Collecting More Informed Opinions of a Population*. Amsterdam: Free University Press, 1987.

O'Neal, Harry "Respondent Cooperation and Industry Image Survey." Unpublished report prepared for the Council for Marketing and Opinion Research, New York, 1996.

Page, Benjamin I. *Choices and Echoes in Presidential Elections: Rational Man in Electoral Democracy*. Chicago: University of Chicago Press, 1978.

Peltzman, Samuel. "Constituent Interest and Congressional Voting." *Journal of Law and Economics* 27(1984): 181–210.

Peterson, Merrill D., ed. *The Portable Thomas Jefferson.* New York: Viking Press, 1975.

Pfiffner, James P. *The Modern Presidency*. New York: St. Martin's Press, 1998.

Poole, Keith. "Dimensions of Interest Group Evaluation of the U.S. Senate, 1969–78." *American Journal of Political Science* 25(1981): 49–67.

Poole, Keith, and Howard Rosenthal. "Patterns of Congressional Voting." *American Journal of Political Science* 35(1991): 228–78.

Popkin, Samuel. *The Reasoning Voter*. Chicago: University of Chicago Press, 1991.

Presser, Stanley, Paul Lavrakas, Vincent Price, and Michael Traugott. "How Do People Decide Whether to Believe the Results of a Poll?" Paper presented at the annual conference of the American Association for Public Opinion Research, St. Louis, 15–17 May 1998.

Preston, Peter. "Race for the White House." *The Guardian* (London), 9 November 2000, 2.

Price, Vincent, and Hayg Oshagan. "Social Psychological Perspectives on Public Opinion." In *Public Opinion and the Communication of Consent*, ed. Theodore Glasser and Charles Salmon. New York: Guilford Press, 1993.

Proffitt, Waldo. "Progress in Campaign Reform." *Sarasota Herald Tribune* 23 February 1987.

Rabinowitz, George, Stuart Macdonald, and Ola Listhaug. "New Players in an Old Game: Party Strategy in Multiparty Systems." *Comparative Political Studies* 24(1991):147–85.

Rahn, Wendy. "Candidate Evaluation in Complex Information Environments: Cognitive Organization and Comparison Process." In *Political Judgment: Structure and Process*, ed. Milton Lodge and Kathleen M. McGraw. Ann Arbor: University of Michigan Press, 1995.

Randall, Willard Sterne. *Thomas Jefferson: A Life.* New York: Henry Holt, 1993.

Randolph, Eleanor. "Journalists Wield Polling Sword at Their Peril." *Los Angeles Times*, 22 February 1996, 19–23

Rasinski, Kenneth A. "The Effect of Question Wording on Public Support for Government Spending." *Public Opinion Quarterl,* 53(1989): 388–94.

Remini, Robert. *Andrew Jackson.* New York: Harper and Row, 1966.

Rich, Frank. "Everybody into the Political Mudfight." *The New York Times*, 26 February 2000, A15.

Roper, Burns W. "Evaluating Polls with Poll Data." *Public Opinion Quarterly,* 50(1986): 10–16.

Rosenthal, Andrew. "Broad Disparities in Votes and Polls Raising Questions." *The New York Times*, 9 November 1981, A1.

Sabato, Larry J., and Glenn R. Simpson. *Dirty Little Secrets: The Persistence of Corruption in American Politics*. New York: Random House, 1996.

Salwen, Michael. "The Reporting of Public Opinion Polls during Presidential Years, 1968–1984." *Journalism Quarterly* 62(1985): 272–77.

Sartori, Giovanni. *The Theory of Democracy Revisited: Part 1, The Contemporary Debate*. Chatham, N.J.: Chatham House, 1987.

Schlesinger, Arthur M., Jr. *The Cycles of American History.* Boston: Houghton Mifflin, 1986.

———. *The Age of Jackson.* Boston: Little, Brown 1945.

Schuman, Howard, and Stanley Presser. *Questions and Answers in Attitude Surveys: Experiments on Question Form, Wording, and Context*. New York: Academic Press, 1986.

Schumpeter, Joseph. *Capitalism, Socialism, and Democracy.* New York: Harper, 1950.

Seligman, Lester G., and Cary R. Covington. *The Coalitional Presidency*. Chicago: Dorsey Press, 1989.

Simendinger, Alexis. "In His Own (Mixed) Words." *National Journal*, 28 April 2001: 1249.

Skocpol, Theda. "The Aftermath of Defeat." *Journal of Health Politics, Policy, and Law* 18(1995): 530–50.

———. "The Rise and Resounding Demise of the Clinton Plan." *Health Affairs* 14(1995): 66–85.

Slaton, Christa Daryl. *Televote: Expanding Citizen Participation in the Quantum Age*. New York: Praeger, 1992.

Smith, Craig Allen. "Redefining the Rhetorical Presidency." In *The Clinton Presidency: Images, Issues, and Communication Strategies*, ed. Robert Denton and Rachael Holloway. Westport, Conn.: Praeger, 1996.

Sniderman, Paul, James Glaser, and Robert Griffin. "Information and Electoral Choice." In *Information and Democratic Processes*, ed. John Ferejohn and James Kuklinkski. Urbana: University of Illinois Press, 1990.

Stephanopoulos, George. *All Too Human: A Political Education*. Boston: Little, Brown, 1999.

Stimson, James A., Michael B. Mackuen, and Robert S. Erikson. "Dynamic Representation." *American Political Science Review* 89(1995): 543–65.

Streb, Matthew J. *The New Electoral Politics of Race*. Tuscaloosa: University of Alabama Press, 2002.

Stuckey, Mary E. *The President as Interpreter-in-Chief*. Chatham, N.J.: Chatham House, 1991.

Sunstein, Cass R. "Deliberative Trouble?: Why Groups Go to Extremes." *Yale Law Journal*, 2000, 110–19.

Tannenbaum, Percy H., and Leslie J. Kostrich. *Turned-On TV / Turned-Off Voters: Policy Opitions for Election Projections*. Beverly Hills, Calif.: Sage, 1983.

Tenpas, Kathryn Dunn, and Stephen Hess. "Bush's A Team: Just Like Clinton's But More So." *Washington Post*, 27 January 2002, B05.

Traugott, Michael W. "Public Attitudes about News Organizations, Campaign Coverage, and Polls." In *Polling and Presidential Election Coverage*, ed. Paul J. Lavrakas and Jack K. Holley Newbury Park, Calif.: Sage Publications, 1991.

———. "The Impact of Media Polls on the Public." In *Media Polls in American Politics*, ed. Thomas E. Mann and Gary R. Orren. Washington, D.C.: The Brookings Institution, 1992.

———. "The Role of the Mass Media in Conveying Public Opinion Accurately." Paper presented at the World Association for Public Opinion Research conference on Data Quality, Cadenabbia, Italy, 24–27 June 1998.

———. "The Invocation of Public Opinion in Congress." Paper presented at the annual meeting of the International Political Science Association, Quebec City, 1–6 August 2000.

———. "Assessing Poll Performance in the 2000 Campaign." *Public Opinion Quarterly* 65(2001): 389–419.

———. "The Nature of a Belief in a Mass Public." In *Electoral Democracy*, ed. Michael MacKuen and George Rabinowitz Ann Arbor: University of Michigan Press, forthcoming.

Traugott, Michael W., and Mee-Eun Kang. "Public Attention to Polls in an Election Year." In *Election Polls, the News Media, and Democracy,* ed. Paul J. Lavrakas and Michael W. Traugott. New York: Chatham House, 2000.

———. "Push Polls as Negative Persuasive Strategies." In *Election Polls, the New Media, and Democracy*, ed. Paul J. Lavrakas and Michael W. Traugott. New York: Chatham House, 2000.

Traugott, Michael W,. and Paul J. Lavrakas. *The Voter's Guide to Election Polls.* Chatham, N.J.: Chatham House, 2000.

Traugott, Michael W., and Elizabeth C. Powers. "Did Public Opinion Support the Contract with America?" In *Election Polls, The News Media, and Democracy*, ed. Paul J. Lavrakas and Michael W. Traugott. New York: Chatham House, 2000.

Traugott, Michael W., and Vincent Price. "Exit Polls in the 1989 Virginia Gubernatorial Race: Where Did They Go Wrong?" *Public Opinion Quarterly* 56(1992): 245–53.

Tulis, Jeffrey K. *The Rhetorical Presidency*. Princeton: Princeton University Press, 1987.

Van Natta, Don, Jr. "Years Ago, Bush Advisor in Texas Helped Draft a Poll Using Disputed Method." *The New York Times*, 15 February 2000, A22.

Verba, Sidney, Kay Lehman Schlozman, and Henry Brady. *Voice and Equality: Civic Volunteerism in American Politics*. Cambridge: Harvard University Press, 1995.

"VNS Chief Reports on Exit Poll." *Associated Press,* 9 May 2001.

Walker, Dave. "Truth or Consequences." *The Times-Picayune*, 29 November 2000, P1.

Wayne, Stephen J. *The Road to the White House, 1996: The Politics of Presidential Elections*. New York: St. Martin's Press, 1996.

———. *The Road to the White House, 2000: The Politics of Presidential Elections*, Postelection edition. Boston: Bedford/St. Martins, 2001.

West, Darrell, Diane Heith, and Chris Goodwin. "Harry and Louise Go to Washington: Political Advertising and Health Care Reform." *The Journal of Health Politics, Policy, and Law* 21(1996):35–68.

Worcester, Robert M. *Journalist's Guide to the Publication of Opinion Survey Results*. London: Market and Opinion Research International, 1987.

Worthington, Peter. "Like Idiots, We Trusted the Box." *Toronto Sun*, 9 November 2000, 16.

Wyer, Robert, Thomas Lee Budesheim, Sharon Shavitt, Ellen Riggle, R. Jeffrey Melton, and James Kuklinski. "Image, Issues, and Ideology: The Processing of Information about Political Candidates." *Journal of Personality and Social Psychology* 52(1991): 196–202.

Yardley, Jim. "Calls to Voters at Center Stage in G.O.P. Race." *The New York Times*, 14 February 2000, A1.

Zeidenstein, Harvey G. "Presidents' Popularity and Their Wins and Losses on Major Issues: Does One Have Greater Influence Over the Other?" *Presidential Studies Quarterly* 15(1985): 287–300.

Contributors

James S. Fishkin is Janet M. Peck Chair in International Communication and Professor of Political Science at Stanford University where he is also Director of the Center for Deliberative Democracy. He is the author of several books including *Democracy and Deliberation: New Directions for Democratic Reform* (Yale University Press, 1991) and *The Voice of the People: Public Opinion and Democracy* (Yale University Press, 1995) and the editor with Peter Laslett of *Debating Deliberative Democracy* (Blackwell, 2003). He originated Deliberative Polling and has conducted more than twenty such experiments in public opinion research in the United States, Britain, Denmark, Australia, Bulgaria and other countries. He holds a Ph.D. in Political Science from Yale and a Ph.D. in Philosophy from Cambridge. He has been a Guggenheim Fellow and a Fellow of the Center for Advanced Study in the Behavioral Sciences at Stanford as well as Visiting Fellow Commoner at Trinity College, Cambridge.

Michael A. Genovese is Loyola Chair of Leadership Studies and Professor of Political Science at Loyola Marymount University. He has written fourteen books, including *The Power of the American Presidency* and *The Paradoxes of the American Presidency*. Dr. Genovese is the editor of *The Encyclopedia of the American Presidency* for Facts-on-File. He has won over a dozen university and national teaching awards.

Diane J. Heith is Assistant Professor of Government and Politics at St. John's University. She is the author of several works on polling and the presidency, including, *Polling to Govern: Public Opinion and Presidential Leadership*. Her work has appeared in *Public Opinion Quarterly, Presidential Studies Quarterly, Political Science Quarterly, White House Studies* and *The Encyclopedia of Public Opinion*. She has also co-authored an article on the health care debate and political advertising for *The Journal of Health Politics, Policy and Law*.

Melinda S. Jackson is a Ph.D. Candidate in the Department of Political Science at the University of Minnesota. Her research interests include political psychology, public opinion, and political identity.

Lawrence R. Jacobs is Professor of Political Science, Adjunct Professor in the Hubert H. Humphrey Institute at the University of Minnesota, and Associate Director of the Institute of Social, Economic, and Ecological Sustainability. He is currently chair of the American Political Science Association's Task Force on Inequality and American Democracy. Dr. Jacobs' most recent book is *Politicians Don't Pander: Political Manipulation and the Loss of Democratic Responsiveness* (with Robert Shapiro), which received the Goldsmith Book Prize from Harvard University's Shorenstein Center for Press and Politics, the Neustadt Book Prize from the American Political Science Association, and the Distinguished Book Prize in political sociology from the American Sociological Association. He also authored, *The Health of Nations: Public Opinion and the Making of Health Policy in the U.S. and Britain* as well as publications in the *American Political Science Review, World Politics, Comparative Politics, Public Opinion Quarterly*, and other scholarly and popular outlets. Dr. Jacobs received a prestigious Robert Wood Johnson Investigator Award in Health Policy Research and grants from the Ford Foundation, National Science Foundation, the Pew Charitable Trusts, the Russell Sage Foundation, the McKnight Foundation, the Robert Wood Johnson Foundation, and others.

Susan H. Pinkus is the Director of the *Los Angeles Times* Poll. She has published articles in *Public Perspective* and *PS*. She is on the Board of Directors at the Roper Center, is a trustee for the National Council on Public Polls (NCPP), and is the past president of the Pacific Chapter of the American Association for Public Opinion Research.

Matthew J. Streb is Assistant Professor of Political Science at Loyola Marymount University. He is the author of *The New Electoral Politics of Race* and co-editor with Christine Barbour of *Clued in to Politics: A Critical Thinking Reader in American Government*. He has published a half dozen articles in journals including *Public Opinion Quarterly, Political Research Quarterly, Social Science Quarterly*, and *Politics and Policy*.

Michael W. Traugott is Professor of Communication Studies and Political Science and Chair of the Department of Communication

Studies at the University of Michigan. The author of 9 books and more than 60 articles and book chapters, his most recent work focused on a revised edition of *The Voter's Guide to Election Polls* and an edited volume, *Election Polls, the News Media, and Democracy*, both with Paul Lavrakas. He is also the author, with Edie Goldenberg, of *Campaigning for Congress*. He is a past president of the American Association for Public Opinion Research, and he was recently selected as a Fellow of the Midwest Association for Public Opinion Research.

Gerald C. Wright is Professor of Political Science at Indiana University. His research interests are in the relationship between public preferences and what governments do. He is the author or co-author of four books including *State House Democracy* and *Keeping the Republic*. Wright has over 40 articles that have appeared in professional journals and as chapters in edited volumes.

Index